Acknowledgments

We are most grateful to the following people for their help in the production of this book: Marilla Dann, Keith Goldsworthy, Tak Nishizawa, Yvonne McDonald, Grant Rylander, Amanda Skull, Brenda Skull , David Skull and John Slater.

We gratefully acknowledge our indebtedness to the following organisations which have allowed us to use their visual material: Ardomona Fruit Products Co-operative; Australian Consolidated Press Ltd.; Australian Pork Corporation; Circulon, Le Cook's-Ware Inc.; Davis Consolidated Industries Ltd. and Davis Gelatine (Australia) Co.; Farmers Union Foods Ltd.; Gakken & Co Ltd., Japan; Kikkoman Corporation; Kraft Foods Ltd; Peck's Australia Ltd.; Matsushita Electrical Industrial; Unifoods Pty Ltd.; National Panasonic (Australia) Pty. Ltd,; Nestlé Australia Ltd.; Rosella Lipton Pty Ltd.; Socomin International Fine Foods and White Wings Foods.

Errata
Page 1 for **NIK-WAZ** read **NEES-WAZ**
Page 43 for **Cajan** read **Cajun**
Page 92 for **fettucine** read **fettuccine**
Page 186 for **ram meaning cheese** read **ram meaning cream**
Page 194 for **rissoto** read **risotto**
Page 201 for **saltimboca** read **saltimbocca**
Page 209 for **scallopine (i)** read **scaloppine or scaloppina**

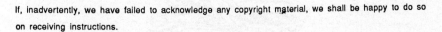

If, inadvertently, we have failed to acknowledge any copyright material, we shall be happy to do so on receiving instructions.

Thought For Food

De gustibus non est disputandum

> *(Latin for - There is no argument regarding taste)*

Chacun à son goût

> *(French for - Each to his/her own taste)*

Good cooking is the basis of true happiness

> *(Auguste Escoffier)*

It's a fundamental fact that no cook, however creative and capable, can produce a dish of quality any higher than that of the raw ingredients.

> *(Alice Waters)*

The appreciation of good food, like the appreciation of good music, is an unmistakable sign of culture.

> *(Lin Yotang)*

Half the eating is in the eye

> *(Portuguese saying)*

À la

Pronounced À LA (with a's as in cat) as in :

à l'Anglaise (AN-GLAZ with the first a as in bat, the second as in date)

à la boulangère (BOO-LAN-JAIR with oo as in soon, a as in cat, j as s in pleasure and ai as in fair)

à la carte (KART with a as in far)

à la Crecy (KRAY-SEE with ay as in say and ee as in see),

à la diable (DEE-ABLA with ee as in see, first a as in palm and final a as in ago) ,

à la financière (FEE-NAHN-SEE-AIR with ee's as in see, ah as a nasalised a in father, ai as in fair)

à la Grecque (GREK with e as in fetch),

à la jardinière (ZHARDON -EE AIR , with zh as s in measure, a as in far, on as in song, ee as in see and air as in fair)

à la Lyonnaise (LEE-ON-AZ , with ee as in see, on as in song and a as in face),

à la meunière (MUN - EE - AIR, with u as in fur, ee as in see, ai as in fair)

à la niçoise (NIK-WAZ with i as in pick, a as in cat),

à la Normande (NORMANDEE with o as in form, a as in man , ee as in see) ,

à la provençale (PROV-ON-SAL with o as in dog, on as in song and a as in cat)

À la Russe (ROOS , with oo as in soon)

Origin & Meaning

À la is French for *in the manner of* , *in the style of, according to, like the*, as in like the Greeks - **à la Grecque**, or simply *with,* as in *with orange* - *à* **l'orange**, *with mustard* - **à la moutard**, *with tomatoes* - **à la tomate**.

Anglaise is French for *English*. **À l' Anglaise** refers to food which has been dipped in beaten egg and then coated with bread crumbs and cooked in butter and oil.

Boulangère is French for *baker*. **À la boulangère** describes a simple dish of stock, potatoes and onions. In days past in France, many households did not have an oven, so housewives took their pies to a local baker to be cooked in his oven.

Carte was originally French for a piece of paper or cardboard and later a bill of fare or menu. **À la carte** means *according to the menu and* what is written down as available on the menu.

One has a selection from all the dishes on the menu, all of which are individually priced; whereas when the menu is **table d'hôte**, a limited choice of dishes is available.

Crecy is a town in France famous for its carrots. **À la Crecy** describes dishes containing mainly carrots.

Diable is French for the *devil* or *Satan*. **À la Diable** means served with a very sharp and hot seasoning.

Financière is French for a *financier* who is involved in the stock-market. That is someone well able to afford the expensive things in life. **À la Financière** describes a very rich sauce, which is often used for entrées, such as bouchées, vol au vents and quenelles. The sauce often includes expensive ingredients such as cocks' combs and truffles.

À la Grecque indicates that the dish has been prepared in the Greek style. That is with lemon, olive oil and fresh herbs, ingredients readily available in Greece.

Jardinière is French for a *gardener* or *from a garden*, as in garden plants. **À la jardinière** describes a dish which has a garnish of garden vegetables, such as carrots, peas, beans and cauliflower, which have been cooked separately. A dish can be

a la Crecy

salad à la niçoise

presented elegantly by arranging each vegetable around a main dish of fish, meat or poultry. Sometimes the garnish is topped with a hollandaise sauce.

Lyonnaise means *from the city of Lyon*, a city in East Central France, which is famous as an onion-growing region. **À la Lyonnaise** in French means *with onions* or served *with Lyonnaise sauce*, which is made from onions, white wine and a meat glaze.(See: **soubise**)

Meunière is French for a *miller's wife* or the *female owner of a flour-mill.* **À la Meunière** means that the dish is served with a sauce of butter (**beurre noisette**), lemon juice and parsley. More often than not, it refers to a fish dish (e.g **sole meunière**) or a seafood dish which is cooked in white wine.

Normande is French for *Normandy* , which is a province in the North West of France, where many apples are grown. **À la Normande** means that the dish has been prepared with a fruit plentiful in Normandy - the apple. The dish is cooked with butter, cream, apples, cider and perhaps with calvados, a liqueur made from apple cider.

Niçoise is French for *from Nice.* **À la niçoise** means originating in Nice, a city in the South of France. The region is noted for its tomatoes, black olives, beans, artichokes, garlic and potatoes, and also for fish, such as tuna and anchovies. Dishes **à la niçoise** usually include these products.

provence, from which **provençal** is derived, is an area in the South of France. **À la provençal** describes a dish which uses products which flourish in the area of Provence, namely tomatoes, onions, garlic and olives.

Russe is French for *Russia.* **À la Russe** describes a dish to which sour cream or beetroot or both are added.

Associations
see: al and alla

Aïoli

Pronounced AYOLEE (with a as in ape, o as in over and ee as in see)

Origin
Aïoli or **ailloli** is from the French *ail* meaning *garlic.* The dish originated either in Greece or in Provence in the South of France. It is now very popular in the South of France, Greece and Spain.

Meaning
Aïoli is made from pounded cloves of garlic, egg yolks, oil and seasoning. It is made by adding olive oil very slowly to the pounded mixture, as in the making of mayonnaise. Just before it is served, lemon juice and a little cold water are added. It is served as a sauce for a variety of garnishes and main courses (such as boiled fish, cooked vegetables or cold meats) or as a strongly-flavoured dip.

Associations
The Italian for aïoli is **aglio,** the Spanish is **ajo** and **allioli.**
see: **crudité, garnish, mayonnaisse**

Al and Alla

Pronounced   AL (*a as in far,*) as in:

al carbonara (KAR BON ARA with the first two a's as in far and the last as in ago and o as in on),
al dente (DEN- TAY with e as in men, ay as in say),
al forno (FORNO, with first o as in for and second o as in go),
al fresco (FRESKO with e as in fresh, o as in go),
ALLA pronounced ALA (both a's as in far), as in :
alla griglia (GREE-LEE-A with ee's as in see and a as in cat)
alla parmigiana (PAM EE -YA -NA with first a as in pan, other two a's as in far, ee as in see),
alla pizzaiola (PEEDZ -I-YOLA with ee as in see, i as in fine, o as in on and a as in far),
alla spiedo (SP'YAY-DO with ay as in say and o as in go)

alla spiedo

Origin & Meaning

These are all Italian words.
Carbonara means *grilled.* **Al carbonara** means   cooked (originally grilled) with diced ham, bacon or belly of pork and eggs.
Dente means *tooth.* **Al dente** means slightly resistant to the bite; that is, it is just soft enough so that the teeth are hardly necessary to break the pasta.
Fresco means *fresh.* **Al fresco** means in a fresh, uncooked manner or to eat out in the open air.
Forno means *oven.* **Al forno** means baked in an oven .

Griglia means a *grill.* **Alla griglia** means cooked on a   grill.
Parmigiana means *parmesan,* which is a very hard, seasoning cheese originally from Parma in North Italy. **Alla Parmigiano** means made with, or dressed with parmesan cheese .
Pizzaiola means *like a small pizza with garlic sauce.* **Alla pizzaiola** means made with tomato sauce, black pepper, oregano

and garlic. (The Italians were the first to cook with tomatoes).
Spiedo means *a spit.* **Alla spiedo** means roasted on a spit.

Associations
see: **à la, au, spaghetti**

Almond

Pronounced AMAND (*a as in far, a as in ago*)

Origin
The word almond derives from the Latin **amygdala** meaning the
kernel of a fruit tree which is much like a peach. It is   native of
Western India and also flourished in the Eastern Mediterranean. It
is mentioned in the Bible and has a very long ancestry. Almonds
have always been an important ingredient in Arabic dishes and
Indian curries. They are now cultivated throughout the world and
they are a major commercial crop in the United States.

almond biscuits

trout with almonds

Meaning

There are two kinds of almonds : **sweet almonds** which are used in cooking and which can be eaten raw (either blanched without skins or with skins) and **bitter almonds** which are usually distilled into an essence (extract) and which are used to some extent in cooking.

Almonds are used in almond cream (such as **frangipane**, a pastry cream) almond milk, almond nougat, almond paste and simply as chopped nuts (raw, roasted, shredded and salted). It is also the main ingredient in **marzipan**, from which many confections are produced. **Almondine**, or **almandine**, describes dishes or confections which are made or garnished with almonds (e.g. **troute almandine**). In France, **amandé** means flavoured with almonds.

Amaretti are Italian **macaroons** made from bitter almonds and **kipfere** or **kippels** are crescent-shaped almond biscuits which are popular in Germany. **Kab el ghzal** are almond crescents enjoyed in North Africa. **Dragées** are sweet almonds coated with hard sugar and **pralines** consist of caramelised sugar flavoured with burnt almonds. **Vienna almonds** are toffee-coated

7

almonds. The Greek **koorabiedes** and the Mexican **torta de cielo** (" cake of heaven") are almond cakes and the Portuguese **tarta de amendoa** is an almond sponge. **Ratafie** or **ratafia** is the essence of bitter almond, an almond biscuit and a liqueur flavoured with almonds. **Condé** is almond icing.

Associations
See: blanc mange, croissant, marzipan, pilaf, pithiviers, semolina, stollen

Antipasto

Pronounced ANTI-PASTO (with a's as in cat , i as in pin and o as in over)

Origin
Anti is Italian for *before* and **pasto** for the *meal*. It literally means *before the meal*, and has come to mean before the main course of the meal.

Meaning
Antipasti (note the plural of the word) are what the French call **hors d'oeuvres**. **Antipasto** consists of a very wide range of vegetables (raw, cooked and pickled), fish, seafood, ham, sausages, olives and bread. What is included depends to some extent on what foods are in season in a particular area.

Associations
See: appetizer, hors d'oeuvre, marinade, mezze, mortadella, **prosciutto,** salami

Appetizer

Pronounced APY -TIZA (first a as in apple, y as in duty, i as in mine and final a as in ago)

Origin
Appetite derives from the Latin **appetere** meaning *to strive after, to seek.* As most people strove to get food, the word became associated with the desire for food or the capacity to eat food. **Appetizer is,** a 20th century extension of the word and has

changed its original meaning to denote something eaten to stimulate the appetite.

devils on horseback

Meaning

An **appetizer** is a small portion of a savoury, piquant dish which is served before a main meal, in order to stimulate the appetite. Appetizers are sometimes called **palate teasers** or what the French call **amuse bouche** or **amuse gueulle** (bouche and gueulle both mean *mouth*).

Associations

In France, a **bonne bouche** is a *titbit*.
see: antipasto, cassolette, caviar, croissant, croustade, croûte, crudité, dim sum, hors d'oeuvre, filo, foie gras, mezze, rillette, rissole, rollmop, samosa, soufflé, spring rolls, spanikopita, tahini, taramasalata, terrine, vol au vent, wurst

Arroz con pollo

Pronounced ARROS -KON -POYO (with a as in cat, first and second o as in cot, third and fourth o's as in go, y as in yes)

Origin
Arroz means *rice*, **con** means *with* and **pollo** means *chicken* in Spanish. This dish has been eaten the length and breadth of Spain since rice was introduced into Spain in the 16th century.

Meaning
Arroz con pollo is a popular Spanish and Mexican dish which is basically chicken and rice. The Spanish prefer short-grained rice for their dishes. Chicken pieces are browned in oil and butter and then added to onions and rice. Chicken stock is added and the dish is simmered for about 30 minutes. Sautéed chicken livers are chopped and green peppers, pimientos, mushrooms and tomatoes are added to the rice and chicken and the cooking continues for about another 10 minutes until the chicken is very tender.

Associations
see: **rice, risotto, poularde**

Aspic

Pronounced ASPIK
(with a as in cat and i as in pick)

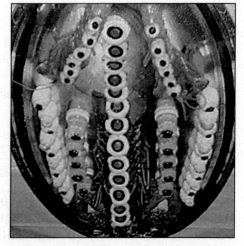

Origin
Some believe that **aspic** is derived from the *asp,* a small serpent-like snake which, as it is very cold, resembles in some respects the jelly of aspic. Others believe that it originated with the Greek word **aspis** meaning a *shield,* as the first moulds for making aspic were in the form of a shield.

Meaning

Aspic consists of a clear or coloured savoury meat jelly into which slices of meat, fish, seafood, vegetables, eggs or fruit are placed. The jelly of sweet aspics can be flavoured with dessert wines or liqueurs. The mixture is placed in a mould (preferably a metal mould as aspic sets more quickly in a metal container than in a china bowl) and refrigerated to set it. The firm, moulded aspic is served as a cold dish. Also aspic jelly can be brushed over cooked meat or poultry (for example a cooked chicken) to give a cold dish an attractive glazed effect.

Associations

see: **ballotine, chaud froid, galantine**

Au
au beurre, au bleu , au fromage, au gratin, au jus, au lait, au naturel, au poivre)

Pronounced -Au - AW (with aw as in saw)
au beurre -BUR (with ur as in fur),
au bleu -BLO (with o as in lemon)
au fromage - FROM -AZH (with o as in go, a as in lard and zh as the **s** sound in measure)
au gratin - GRAT-AHN (with a as in fat, and ah with a nasal sound)
au jus - JOOS (with oo as in moon),
au lait - LAY (with ay as in say),
au naturel - NA- TUR - EL (with a as in fat, ur as in tureen, and el as in bell),
au poivre - PWA- VRA (with first a as in star and final a as in ago and all the consonants sounded

Origin & Meaning

Au is French and has the same meaning as **à la**. It can be translated as *in* (e.g. in butter), *with* (e.g. with milk) or *made with* (e.g. made with cheese). In French, **beurre** means *butter*, and **au beurre** means made with or in butter.
Bleu means *blue* and **au bleu** describes the process where freshly-killed fish (e.g. trout) is plunged into boiling water and

poached until the skin of the fish has a bluish tinge. The fish is then cooked in fish stock and wine.

Fromage means *cheese* and **au fromage** means made with or in cheese.

Gratin means *seasoned bread-crumbs* and **au gratin** means cooked (usually grilled/broiled) with seasoned bread crumbs covering the dish, so that the finished dish has a golden crust on it. Nowadays, cheese is also used to coat a **gratihéed** dish.

Jus means *juice* and **au jus** means cooked in its own juice or sauce.

Lait means *milk* and **au lait** means *with milk* (as in *café au lait*).

naturel means *natural (simple)* and **au naturel** means *in its natural state.* It refers to foods which are served very simply or which are uncooked (e.g. **oysters au naturel**).

Poivre means *pepper* and **au poivre** means cooked with pepper, as in *steak au poivre.*

Associations
see: **à la, al** and **alla, coulis**

Avgolemono

Pronounced   AVGO-LEMONO (with a as in cat, first o as in go, e as in pet and the other two o's as in on)

Origin
Avgo is Greek for *egg* and **lemono** for *lemon*. It literally means *egg-lemon*.

Meaning
Avgolemono is chicken broth or stock flavoured with lemon juice and whipped into a frothy blend with eggs. It is seasoned and then often thickened with long-grained rice. The smooth-textured soup with a refreshing tart flavour is served cold while still foaming. It is sometimes used to flavour other soups or is served with fish, poultry or vegetables.

Associations
A popular dish in Greece and Turkey is lamb with spinach and avgolemono sauce. It is called **arni me spanaki avgolemono.**
see: vichyssoise

Baba

Pronounced   BABA (*with a's as in far*)

Origin
The **baba** is said to have originated with King Stanislas Leczinski of Poland, the father-in-law of King Louis XV of France, who sprinkled a **kugelhopf** (a **yeast cake**) with rum and set it alight. The new cake was a great success and, as the king enjoyed reading the "*Thousand and One Nights*" stories, King Stanislas named the new cake after one of its heroes, *Ali Baba.* The Ancient Egyptians were the first to discover that fermenting dough (using yeast) produces gases in bread and pastries which makes them softer and lighter than when yeastless dough is used.

Meaning
A **baba** is rich cake made with yeast dough and raisins,which is baked in a **dariol** (a cylindrical mould), which is lined with shredded almonds. The cake is then steeped or flavoured according to one's taste) in a rum or kirsch (a cherry brandy)

syrup or a desssert wine. Fruit is sometimes used as a garnish, in which case the baba takes its name from the fruit, e.g. **pineapple baba** or **apricot baba**. In France, it is also called a **pâte à baba** or a **baba au rhum**.

babas

Associations
see: **dessert, gâteau, kugelhopf, savarin**

Bagel

Pronounced BAGAL (with first a as in ape and second as in ago)

Origin
Bagel derives from the Yiddish **beygl**, which comes from the German **beugel** meaning a *bracelet*.

Meaning

Bagels are breadrolls in the shape of a doughnut or an old-fashioned curtain ring. A brown and glossy crust is obtained on the rolls by first boiling them in water and then baking them in an oven. Sometimes they are filled with cream cheese and smoked salmon to make a delicious snack.

bagel with egg, ham and salad

Associations

In French cuisine, the word **echaudé** (AY-SHO-DAY - *with ay's as in say and o as in over*) means *to scald* or to poach dough first in an oven and then bake it dry.

Bagna cauda

Pronounced BAGNA COWDA (with a's as in bag and ow as in cow)

Origin

Bagna is Italian for sauce or gravy and **cauda** for *hot*. It literally means *hot sauce*. Both the words are dialect words from Piedmont. The dish is a traditional speciality of the Piedmont district of North West Italy (whose capital is Turin).

Meaning

Bagna cauda (or caôda) is a hot dip made from crushed anchovies, butter, garlic and olive oil. Usually, there is a communal dish in the middle of a table containing the sauce. The sauce is cooked at the table and kept hot. Crisp raw vegetables (**crudités**), such as tomatoes, cardoons (a kind of artichoke) celery, peppers and lettuce, and bread sticks (**grissini**) are dipped into the hot sauce.

Associations
see: **crudités, grissini, sukiyaki**

Baguette

Pronounced BA-GET (with a as in bag and e as in pet)

Origin
Baguette is French for a *rod, wand* or *stick.*

Meaning
In France, **baguette** describes a long, flattened, crispy loaf of bread, which is probably the most popular form of bread in France. Often it is cut crosswise into two or three pieces and used for sandwiches.

Bain marie

Pronounced BAH - MAREE (*with ah said through the nose, a as in far and ee as in see*)

Origin
Bain is French for *bath* and **Marie** for the name *Maria* or *Mary.*
The **bain marie** is a cooking utensil which was invented by an Italian alchemist Maria di Cleofa. She invented it while engaged in research on a treatise involving magic, medicine and cooking. The pan became known as a **bagno maria** (*Maria's bath*). It was later used in France, where it went under the name with the same meaning in French - **bain Marie**.

Meaning

A bain marie is a fairly-large pan (or tray) which is partly filled with water. Food in another vessel is placed in the pan, in order that the food is not cooked too quickly or harshly. Food such as egg custards, custard creams, blanc mange, butter sauces and mousses, which may turn "oily" or fall apart if

a modern bain marie

cooked on a direct heat, can be safely cooked in a bain marie. It is also used to keep food warm after it has been cooked and taken from an oven.

Associations

The term **double-boiler** is used in some countries (e.g. in the U.S.A. and the United Kingdom) for this utensil.
See: **blanc-mange, couscous, hollandaise, oeuf en cocottes, sabayan, semolina, terrine, zabaglione**

Ballottine

Pronounced BALA -TEEN (with 1st a as in cat , 2nd as in ago and ee as in see)

Origin

Balott in French means *a bundle* and **ballotine** *a small bundle*. **Balottine** means a *dish of cold meat bundles or meatballs*.

Meaning

A **ballottine** consists of poultry or game (e.g. a small bird or the leg of a bird) and meat which is boned, then stuffed before being rolled into a bundle shape. It is often coated with **chaud-froid**, glazed in **aspic**, decorated and served cold .

Associations

A **balottine** is very similar to a **galantine**.
See: **aspic, chaud-froid, galantine, paupiette**

Barquette

Pronounced BA - KET (with a as in far, e as in pet)

Origin
Barque is French for *boat* and ***barquette*** for a *little boat.*

Meaning
Barquettes are pastries in the shape of little oval boats. Usually they are baked blind (*empty*) and then they are filled with either a savoury or (more often) a sweet filling, e.g. **barquette au rhum** and **barquette au miel** (with honey). They are served as snacks, desserts or as hors d'oeuvres or small entrées, either hot or cold.

Associations
See: **cassolette entrée, hors d'oeuvre , vol au vent**

Bavarois

Pronounced BAVA-RWA (with a's as in cat and all the consonants sounded)

Origin
Bavarois is French for *from Bavaria* in South Germany, whose capital is Munich. The name of the dish, **bavarois**, was first used by a French chef who worked in Bavaria.

Meaning
A **bavarois** is a cold dessert which is made in a mould. It consists of eggs, cream or custard, gelatin to set it and something to give it strong flavour, such as chocolate, coffee, liqueur or a fruit purée. It is also called a **bavarian cream** or **crème bavaroise** and in Germany **Bayerische vanille creme**.
Bavarois should not be confused with a **bavaroise**, which is a beverage made of tea, capillary or clarified sugar (and an egg yolk sometimes), milk and sometimes lemon or vanilla flavouring.

Associations
A **rondin** is like a bavarois but in the shape of a log.
See: **blanc mange, charlotte, dessert**

Béarnaise

Pronounced
BAIR -NAZ with ai as in fair, a as in day)

Origin
Béarnaise is named after Béarn, a region in the Pyrenees mountain range in South West France, where the sauce was first made.

Meaning
Béarnaise sauce is one of almost 200 French sauces which vary in their appearance and taste. It is a variation of **Hollandaise sauce**. White wine or vinegar, diced shallots, tarragon (which is essential) and peppercorns are reduced and sieved and then added to hollandaise sauce. The sauce gets most of its distinctive taste from the spice tarragon, which has an astringent flavour, something like anise or licorice. The sauce is served with beef, grilled steaks and some shellfish, such as prawns.

Bearnaise sauce

Associations
See: chateaubriand, hollandaise

Béchamel

Pronounced   BE -CHA -MEL (with e's as in let and a as in ago)

Origin
The French version for the derivation of **Béchamel** (or **béchamelle**) sauce is that it was named after Louis de Béchameil, Marquis of Nointel and the Lord Steward of the Royal Household in the court of King Louis XIV of France (1636 - 1715). The Italian version is that it was made in the 14th century and was used by Catharine de Medici (1519-1589), the Italian wife of Henry 11 of France, not only as a sauce but also as a face cream!

Meaning
Béchamel sauce is one of the four basic sauces (called **sauce mères** or **mother sauces** in France) from which all other sauces derive. It is a smooth, white sauce made from finely-chopped vegetables and herbs which are infused in milk and thickened with a roux made with flour or potato flour (**fécule** in French) , boiled milk and butter. It is usually served with white meats, eggs and vegetables. It forms the basis of many other sauces, including aurora, chaudfroid, Lyonnaise, mornay, soubise and tartare.

Associations
The Italian for **béchamel** is **balsamella**.
See: brochette (atteran), chaud-froid, croquette, mornay sauce, roux, soubise, velouté, vol au vent

---

Beef Wellington

Pronounced   BEEF WELINTAN (with ee as in see, e as in let, i as in pin and a as in ago)

Origin
Beef Wellington was named in the mid 19th century in honour of the Duke of Wellington, who was Prime Minister of Britain from 1828 to 1826 but who is best known for his military victory over Napoleon at the battle of Waterloo in 1815.

Meaning

To make **beef Wellington,** a choice fillet of beef (often flambéed in brandy) is covered with liver pâté and sliced mushrooms. The meat is placed in a case of puff pastry and baked in a hot oven.

Associations

Schwein in mantel is a German dish in which a pork fillet is cooked in a pastry case.

see: feuilletage, fillet

Beignet

Pronounced   BAY-NAY (with ay as in say)

Origin

Beignet is French for *fritter*, which comes from the Latin **frigere** meaning *to fry*.

Meaning
Beignet usually refers to a fruit fritter but it also describes a fish, seafood, or vegetable fritter. The fritter is coated with a batter (In France, it is called **pâte à frire** or **beignet batter**) and is deep fried in very hot oil. **Beignet** is also used to describe a small piece of choux pastry which is fried in deep fat and then is rolled in sugar or a savoury sauce and chopped cheese. A popular Latin American dessert is **beignet de bananes**, banana fritter.

Associations
Bunuelos is Spanish for fritter. **Pakorha** are Indian fritters.

Beurre - blanc, maître d'hôtel, manié, noire, noisette, rouge

Pronounced
Beurre - BUR (u as in fur), **blanc** - BLON (on as in long, naselised), **maître** -MAITRA (ai as in fair, a as in ago), **d'hôtel** -DO-TEL (o as in go, el as in bell), **manié** - MANEE-AY (a as in man, ee as in see, ay as in say), **noire** - NWA (with a as in palm), **noisette** - NWA -ZET (a as in cat, e as in net), **rouge** -ROOZH (oo as in moon, zh as s in measure)

Origin & Meaning
In French, **beurre** means *butter*. **Beurres** or **butters** are used as sauces for grills and fish dishes, as garnishes for meats, to improve the flavour of sauces and to make canapés.
Blanc means *white*. **Beurre blanc** originated in the Loire

Valley in France and was at first a sauce for the pike fish caught in the rivers there. **Beurre blanc** is comprised of white wine vinegar which is reduced and then shallots are added. The mixture is thickened with butter.

Maître is French for *master* or *person in charge*. A **maître d'hôtel** in a restaurant is the head waiter. To make **beurre maître d'hôtel**, butter is beaten until it is very creamy and chopped parsley, thyme and lemon juice are added. The mixture is placed on foil, which is folded and rolled to form a sausage shape. It is chilled until firm and then can be cut in round slices. It is often served on grilled meats and fish.

Manié comes from the French verb *manier* meaning *to handle* and **manié** means *kneaded* (with one's hands). **Beurre manié** comprises equal amounts of butter and flour which are kneaded. The paste is added bit by bit and then beaten into a casserole, stew or sauce to thicken it .

Noir means *black* in French and **Beurre noir** is **black butter sauce**. Butter is heated slowly until it is brown and then lemon juice or vinegar, finely-chopped parsley and capers and seasoning are added. It is whisked and the foaming butter is poured over fish (It is particularly associated with skate), sweetbreads or other dishes.

Noisette means hazelnut (brown). **Beurre noisette** is butter that is heated slowly until is a light brown, hazelnut colour. It is then served immediately to accompany a dish, or is used to baste a meat dish.

Rouge means *red.* **Beurre rouge** is the same as **beurre blanc** except that red rather than white wine is used.

There are many kinds of savoury butters, such as anchovy butter, basil butter, cheese butter, crab butter, devilled butter, dill butter, fines herbes butter, garlic butter, horseradish butter, mustard butter and shallot butter.

Associations
See: chateaubriand, roux

brandy butter

Bigarade Sauce

Pronounced BIGARAD (with i
as in big and a's as in cat)

Origin
Bigarade is French for a
bitter-tasting orange from Seville
which is a province in Spain,whose
principal city is also called
Seville.

Meaning
Bigarade sauce, or **orange**
sauce as it is also called, is
made by adding the rind (zest) of
a bitter orange (without any white pith) to reduced **Espagnole**
sauce. It should be strained and reheated with lemon juice and a
little claret or port and some Grand Marnier or other orange
liqueur. Seasoning is then added. Traditionally, the bigarade is
served with goose, quail, roast duck and duckling and pork.

Associations
See: Espagnole sauce

Biriani

Pronounced BIRI-ANI (with i's as in pin and a as in far)

Origin
Biriani derives from the Hindi **biryani** and the Persian
biryan meaning *fried* or *roasted.*

Meaning
Biriani (also spelled **biryani** and **biriyani**) is an Indian dish
made with a **masala** (a spice mixture) which is then coloured
and flavoured with saffron. It is cooked with lamb, chicken, beef
or prawns and it often has alternate layers of rice (pilaf), meat
and spiced garnishes, so that the flavours are blended. A
tablespoon of rosewater, a favourite flavouring in India and the
Middle East, is often added to the dish.

Associations
see: **garam masala, pilaf**

Biscuit

Pronounced BIS-KIT (i's as in bit)

Origin

Biscuit comes the French **bis** meaning *twice* and **cuit** meaning *cooked*. The term originates from **pain bis-cuit** meaning *bread twice cooked.* Twice cooked bread was a staple of the diet of many armies, sailors, travellers and adventurers about two centuries ago, as the sliced, twice - baked bread was light, dry and resistant to spoilage.

Meaning

Basically, biscuits are pieces of dough made from flour, water, sugar and baking powder, plus some shortening. There are three categories of biscuit. First, the **drop biscuit** where the dough is dropped from a spoon onto a baking-tray and then baked (e.g.

kiss cakes, nutties, angel biscuits). Second, **rolled biscuits** where dough is rolled into a thick sheet, cut with a sharp knife and then baked (e.g. gingernuts, vanilla biscuits, lemon biscuits). Third, **sheet biscuits,** where the mixture is placed in a greased baking dish, baked and then cut into a variety of shapes (e.g. almond fingers, caramel fingers). Nowadays, there are hundreds of different biscuits of varied shapes, and textures (e.g crisp, flakey, soft) and often with fillings, such as creams, and jams. The French also have a confection called a **biscuit,** which consists of an ice cream mixture which is cut to look like a biscuit.

Associations
In the U.S.A., **biscuits** are called **cookies** or **crackers,** in Italy **dolci** describes biscuits and cakes. A well-known biscuit from Switzerland is a rectangular spiced biscuit about one centimetre thick called a **leckerli.** Popular biscuits in Europe are **tuiles** (meaning *tiles*) which are wafer-thin biscuits with curled edges which are made from egg whites, castor sugar, flour, butter, vanilla essence, cocoa and milk. A **mazo** is a biscuit of unleavened dough eaten by Jews during the Feast of the Passover. A popular biscuit in Spain is the **polvorones,** made with almonds, cinammon and orange juice.
Biscotto is the Italian and **galleta** the Spanish for a sweet biscuit.
see: florentine

Bisque

Pronounced BISK (with i as in pin)

Origin
Bisque in French means a *shellfish soup.* The word is a corruption of **biscuit,** as the soup was cooked twice to thicken it. Bisques in the 18th century were made of poultry and game, not with shellfish as they usually are today.

Meaning
A **bisque** is a thick, rich, creamy sauce in the form of a purée. To a court bouillon, a roux of creamy butter and pounded fish is added to thicken it. Crushed and powdered shells are sometimes added and the mixture is sieved. Nowadays, shredded shellfish

(such as lobster, prawns, shrimp, or crayfish) are added to the purée. Occasionally, it includes puréed vegetables. Often the bisques are highly spiced. Tomato purée is sometimes added to the bisque to colour it.

Associations
see: **bouillon, chowder, crustacean, purée, velouté**

Blanc-mange

Pronounced BLON - MONZH (*with on's as in song naselised and zh as the s in pleasure*)

Origin
Blanc is French for *white* and **mange** comes from **manger** meaning *to eat* and also *food.* *Blancmange* means literally *white food.* Originally it was a kind of almond cream.

Meaning
Traditionally, **blancmange** is made by pounding a mixture of sweet and bitter almonds into a paste with a little water. This paste is diluted with water and the liquid is then strained to obtain what is called **almond milk.** (If this process is too time-consuming, vanilla essence may be substituted). Sugar is added to softened **gelatine** in a **bain marie** (double boiler) and the almond milk is then added gradually to this mixture, stirring slowly and continuously until the blanc mange has a creamy, delicate texture and is free of even tiny lumps. When the liquid is tepid, a little rum or kirsch may be added , if desired. The cold mixture is then put into a **bavarois** mould to set. It can be served alone or accompany stewed fruit or a conserve as a dessert.

Associations
In the U.S.A., cornstarch (cornflour) is used in the making of blancmange and the dish is sometimes called **cornstarch pudding.**
see: **almond, bain marie, bavarois, dessert**

Blanquette

Pronounced
BLON -KET with on as in song and nasalised and e as in get)

Origin
Blanquette originated with the French word **blanc** meaning *white*. It means a white - coloured stew.

Meaning
Blanquette means a white **fricassée** (stew) or **ragoût** made from the diced white meat of veal, rabbit lamb and chicken, together with egg yolks and cream to bind the ingredients. It is accompanied by mushrooms and tiny onions cooked in a **courtbouillon**.

Associations
see: **bouillon, fricassée, ragoût**

Blini

Pronounced
BLINI (with i's as in pin)

Origin
Blinis are Russian **pancakes**. They have been made in Russia for hundreds of years.

Meaning
A **blini** is a pancake made with yeast and buckwheat flour. It is usually served with cream and, on special occasions, with salmon, caviar, chopped eggs or hollandaise sauce.

Associations
see: **blintz, caviar, crêpe, hollandaise, hors d'oeuvre**

Blintz

Pronounced
BLINTZ (to rhyme with chintz, with i as in pin)

Origin

The **blintz** is a Russian pancake which originated in the Ukraine in Russia (the U.S.S.R.). It was eaten mainly by Jews there. The word derives from the Yiddish **blintse** which comes from the Russian **blinets** which is a small **blini**.

Meaning
A **blintz** is a light, thin pancake which is fried in butter and filled with a sweet or savoury filling (e.g. ricotta or cottage cheese, seasoning and spices or a duxelle, or jam and sour cream) and then folded into a parcel, which may or may not be covered with a sweet or savoury garnish.

Associations
see: **blini, crêpe, duxelle**

Boeuf Bourguinonne

Pronounced BURF (with u as in fur) BOOR-GEE-NON (with oo as in soon, g as in get, ee as in see and o as a naselised o in song)

Origin

Boeuf is Old French for ox, bull or cow. It then also took on the meaning of the flesh of these animals. **Bourgogne** is the French for *Burgundy*, which is a province in the Central West of France, whose capital is Dijon (famous for, among other things, its mustard). The area is renowned for its fine wines, especially its red wines. **Bourguinonne** means *from Burgundy* or *Burgundian.*

Meaning

Bourguinonne sauce (made from onions, bacon, thyme, bay leaf, garlic, seasoning and, above all, a good red wine) is the basis of **beef bourguinonne.** Diced beef is cooked in the sauce and then served surrounded by croûtons.

Associations

In Italy, beef cooked in red wine is called **carbonata.**
see: **casserole, croûton**

Boeuf Stroganoff

Pronounced BURF (with u as in fur) STROGANOF (with o as in dog, a as in ago and o as in orange)

Origin

Boeuf is French for *beef.* The dish **boeuf Stroganoff** was first made in the late 1800's by the chef of Count Stroganoff, a member of the Russian aristocracy.

Meaning

To make **boeuf** (or **bef**) **Stroganoff,** fillet steak in strips of about 1 cm by 5 cms and chopped onions are fried in butter. Having been cored and de-seeded, peppers cut in strips and chopped mushrooms are added to the pan and all the ingredients are fried. Seasoning and tomato paste are then added. Sour

cream is then stirred in slowly and carefully with controlled moderate heat so that the cream does not curdle. The finished dish is garnished with chopped parsley. The dish can be served with rice or noodles.

Associations
Bulgogni, one of Korea's best-known dishes, uses strips of marinated beef with vegetables.
see: fillet

Bolognese

Pronounced BOLO -NAYZ (o's as in dog, ay as in say)

Origin
Bolognese describes food from the city of Bologna, which is the chief city in the region of Emilia-Romagna in Northern

Italy. The city is famous as the centre of a sausage-producing region, especially the large, tasty sausage called **mortadella**. It is also well known for its **pasta**, especially **tagliatelle**, and for the rich sauce (**ragu** or **ragoût**) which often accompanies it. **Spaghetti bolognaise** is one of the the best- known of all Italian dishes outside Italy.

Meaning

Bolognese sauce (called **salsa alla Bolognese** or **ragu Bolognese** in Italy) is made by sautéeing onions, mushrooms and minced beef in hot oil. Tinned or fresh tomatoes are then added with a liberal amount of tomato paste. The mixture is seasoned with a prepared bolognese herb mixture or with fresh or dried oregano, thyme and basil. A beef or chicken stock cube is then crumbled into the dish and salt and pepper to taste added. Some cooks also like to include a teaspoonful of soya sauce. The dish should be simmered slowly for about an hour to an hour and a half. When the sauce is used for spaghetti bolognese, grated parmesan cheese is used as a garnish.

Associations

see: mortadella, parmigiano, pasta, ragoût, spaghetti, tagliatelle

spaghetti bolognese

Bombe

Origin

Bombe is French for a *bomb*. which was used in a cannon. In France, they had at one time a spherical mould for food shaped like a round bomb. Originally, it was made of copper and had a tight lid, so that it could be buried with its contents in salted ice to keep the contents frozen. From this originated the name of an iced pudding, which they called **bombe glacée** (**glace** being the French for ice). Bombe moulds nowadays  have changed and sometimes have intricate and fanciful shapes.

Meaning

The dessert called a **bombe** is made with two different ice cream mixtures. The first is a simple plain ice cream which is used to line a mould casing. The second is a more elaborate ice cream mixture, usually with a strong flavouring, which is used as a filling A bombe is usually decorated when it is complete with crystallised fruit. A bombe is frozen and served cold as a dessert. A well-known and spectacular dessert is the **bombe Alaska or Baked Aklaska** (also called a **Norwegian omelette or Omelette Surprise**). This consists of very hard ice cream which is surrounded by a meringue. It is placed in a hot oven and the meringue can be cooked before the ice cream melts.

Associations

see: **cassata, dessert, parfait**

Bon appetit

Pronounced BO -NAPATEE (with o as in o in a nasalised song, first a as in cat and second as in ago and ee as in see)

Origin
Bon appetit is French for *good apppetite.*

Meaning
There is no similar expression to **bon appetit** in English, except *I hope you enjoy your meal.* Similar expressions in other countries are:

Italy - **buon appetito**; Spain, Mexico and South America - **buen provecho**; Germany - **gesegnete mahlkzeit** (literally *blessed mealtime*) and *guten appetit;* Indonesian - *selamat makan* (literally *good eating*); Greece - *kali orexi.* In Japan it is polite to say to a guest: **Doozo takusan meshiagatte kudasai** which means *please eat a lot .*

Associations
Expressions used when toasting a friend or relative at a meal are*:* French - *à votre santé (to your health),* Spanish - *a vostra saluté;* German - **gesundheit** or **hoch** (*health!).*

Bonne femme

Pronounced BON FAM (with o as in gone, and a as in lamb)

Origin
Bonne is French for *good* and **femme** for *woman.* **Bonne femme** came to mean a simple, good -natured woman.

Meaning
Bonne femme is a term in French cuisine   meaning *cooked in a very simple way,* using the fresh foods found in a particular locality at a certain season, as would a country housewife. Dishes, such as cassseroles and stews, usually have a simple garnish of fresh vegetables (usually including mushrooms and onions) common , fresh herbs and perhaps bacon. **Soupe** (or **potage**) **à la bonne femme** is broth consisting of brown stock, potatoes, mushrooms, onions, leeks, nutmeg and seasoning. A famous dish is **sole bonne femme** which is sole cooked in white wine or milk with a simple white sauce and garnished with strips of mushrooms and piped potatoes.

Associations
see: casserole, navarin, pomme, poularde, ragoût

Bordelaise

Pronounced BORDA -LAYZ (with o as in form, a as in ago and ay as in say)

Origin
Bordelaise is French for *of* or *related to Bordeaux,* which is a province in the South West of France. The area produces some of the finest wines and food of France.

Meaning
Sauce Bordelaise is a sauce made by reducing chopped shallots, pepper,and Bordeaux wine and adding it to **Espagnole**

sauce. A meat glaze, and herbs (e.g. tarragon) are then added It is often served with grilled rump or other steak, which is frequently garnished with marrow from beef bones and chopped parsley.

Associations
see: **crustacean (oysters), Espagnole sauce, garnish**

Borsch

Pronounced BORSH (with o as in form)

Origin
Borsch is from the Russian **borshch** meaning a hearty soup. It is the national soup of the Ukraine in Russia (U.S.S.R.). **Beetroot**, an essential ingredient in the soup called **borsch**, has been grown since pre-historic times. The Ancient Romans used only the leaves of beetroot for food and used the root for medicinal purposes. The root plant was developed as a vegetable in the Mediterranean area in the 15th century.

Meaning
Borsch (or **bôrtsch**) is a highly-seasoned soup made from a wide range of vegetables (what is available to the cook) but beetroot is essential, which gives the soup its characteristic red colour. Chopped ham and sausages are optional additions. When the soup is ready to serve, sour cream is put on top with a sprinkling of finely-chopped parsley and dill. The soup can be served either hot or cold.

Bouchée

Pronounced BOO-SHAY (with oo as in moon and ay as in say)

Origin
Bouchée in French means *a mouthful. Mangez en une bouchée* means *take a bite.*

Meaning
A **bouchée** is a small **pattie** or **puff pastry,** sufficient for a mouthful. It is usually a small puff pastry in the shape of a cup which is baked *blind* (empty) and then filled with a savoury or sweet filling

Associations
see: **appetizer, hors d'oeuvre, vol   au vent**

Bouillabaisse

Pronounced   BOO-YA-BAYS
(with oo as in soon, a as in cat and   ay as in say)

Origin
In French, **bouillir** means *to boil* and **baisse** means a *fall.* The word **bouillabaise** describes the thickening   process (as the level of the liquid falls) of the soup as it boils in its stock. **Bouillabaise** originated in the fishing port of Marseilles in the South of France. It is now made   along the south coast   of France and each area has its own version of the dish.

Meaning
Bouillabaisse, which is probably the most famous of all fish soups, is made from a wide variety of fish and seafood which are cut into uniform size. To the fish are added   onions, chopped tomatoes, herbs   (such as sprigs of fennel, thyme, bay leaf, parsley), garlic and a piece of dry orange peel. A little oil and seasoning are then added and the casserole is then cooked for about

a quarter of an hour. The dish should not be overcooked and should be served piping hot. In France, saffron is a traditional flavouring for bouillabaise.

Associations
A soup containing fish in Italy is called a **brodetto** and a well-known one from Genoa is **ciuppin**. **Zarzuela** is a Spanish fish or shellfish soup. **Waterzooi de poisson** is a French mixed - fish soup. Popular fish soups in Greece are **kakavia** and **psarosoupa** and in Mexico **vatapa**.
see: **casserole, crustacean**

Bouillon

Pronounced BOO-YON (with oo as in soon and on as in song)

Origin
In French a **bouillon** is a transparent **bubble** given off by a boiling liquid and **bouilli** means *boiled*. In cuisine, it originally means a plain, white stock. Today, it means a clear soup or broth made with meat, vegetables or fish   or a meat stock .
Court bouillon derives from **court** which is French for *short* and **bouillon** for a *clear soup* or *meat stock* . It came to mean a liquor, which could be prepared in a fairly short time, which could be used to cook fish.

Meaning
Bouillon is clear soup, often made from beef or chicken. It often forms the basic stock for clear and thickened soups and sauces. The simple bouillon has changed over time by the addition of vegetables which describe the soup. **Bouillon brunoise** has diced vegetables in the soup; **bouillon julienne** has strips of vegetables and **bouillon paysanne** has sliced vegetables added to the broth. **Consommé** is clarified bouillon.
A **court bouillon** is normally used to poach oily fish, such as trout, salmon or shellfish. It consists of water, white wine or vinegar, carrots, onions, thyme, parsley, a bay leaf and salt and peppercorn. This highly-seasoned liquid is boiled before fish or shellfish are added. The slight acidity of the stock helps to retain the texture and flavour of the fish.

Associations
A **bouillon** is also the French name for a little restaurant

serving fixed-price meals and with a small à la carte menu.
see: consommé, dashi, stock

Bouquet garni

Pronounced BOO-KAY (with oo as in moon and ay as in say),
GARNEE (with a as in far and ee as in see)

Origin
In French, **bouquet** means *tuft, bunch* or *nosegay.* **Garni** comes
from the verb **garnir** meaning *to fortify* or *to provide
protection.* It came to mean anything that was provided to
embellish or adorn something and then food which was added to a
dish to decorate it or to make it palatable.

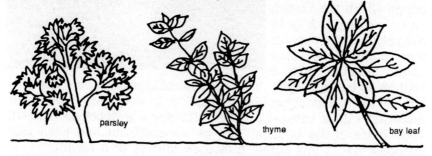

parsley   thyme   bay leaf

Meaning
A **bouquet garni** is a small bunch of herbs, which usually
consists of a basis of sprigs of parsley and thyme and a bay leaf.
Other herbs, such as marjoram, tarragon, cloves, peppercorn,
chervil and rosemary may be added, which complement but do not
dominate the flavours of specific dishes. The herbs and spices are
usually tied in a piece of muslin or they can be enclosed between
the curves of lengths of celery or inserted into slits in leeks.
They are put into stews, casseroles and sauces to flavour them.
The herbs should be fresh, otherwise they go musty. As the
bouquet garni is in a bundle with a string attached, it can be
easily removed from a cooking dish before the dish is ready to be
served.

Associations
A **bouquet garni** is sometimes called a **faggot** in the United
kingdom.
see:casserole, garnish, paupiette, ratatouille

Brioche

BREE-OSH (with ee as
in see and o as in got)

Origin
Brioche is a French
word meaning a *bun* or
cake.

Meaning
A **brioche** is a baked
yeast bread made from
dough which the French
call **pâte à la
brioche.** Originally, it
was in the form of a
small pyramid with a

knot on its top but now it is in various shapes such as a loaf or a
bun or even a doughnut. In France, it is frequently served for
breakfast with a conserve. It can also make a delicious dessert.
The centre of the brioche can be scooped out and filled with
chopped fruit, a fruit purée, a mousse mixture or a cream.

Associations
Coulibiac (or **Koulibiac**) is a Russian dish where a mixture of
finely-chopped sautéed onions and mushrooms and fresh or tinned
salmon is placed on a brioche paste and then the mixture is
covered with thinly-sliced eggs and boiled rice. The brioche is
sealed and then baked until golden brown.
see: dessert, mousse, pâte, purée

Brochette

Pronounced BRO-SHET (with o as in over and et as in met)

Origin
Broche is French for a *spit, spindle* or *skewer.* **Ette** is a
suffix to indicate *smallness.* **Brochette** means a *small skewer.*

Meaning
A **brochette** is a skewered piece of cooked meat. The phrase **en brochette** in French means *skewered.* It is the French term for what in the Middle East is called a **shish kebab** or a **shashlik.**

Associations
In French **à la broche** means *cooked on a spit.* In Italian, it is **allo spiedo.** An **atteran** is a small skewer of cubes of chicken or shellfish with ham and mushrooms. It is coated with béchamel sauce then dipped in egg and bread crumbs and fried in hot fat. It is served as an hors d'oeuvre
see: béchamel sauce, hors d'oeuvre, kebab, satay

Burghul

Pronounced   BUR-GAL (with u as in fur and a as in ago)

Origin
Burghul is derived from the Persian (now Iranian) word **burgul.** In Turkish it is **bulgur.** It means whole wheat which is cooked, dried and cracked. It has been used for pilaf and salads in the Middle East for hundreds of years.

Meaning
Burghul (or **bulgur**) is a cereal where the whole grain of wheat is used. The grain is steamed until partially cooked and dried and the outside bran particles are removed and the grain is cracked. The grain may be fine, medium or full grain and of a light or dark colour depending upon the wheat used. In Midddle East countries, India and in Russia, the grain is mixed with ground lamb or beef, onions, seasoning and spices to make baked **kibbeh**, a speciality of Syria, Lebanon, Kurdistan and parts of Russia. It is also served with **kebabs, pilafs, dolmades** and **salads.**

Associations

Tabouli (also spelled **tabouleh** or **tabbouleh**) consists of a mixture of burghul, mint, parsley, tomatoes, chopped spring onions, lemon juice, olive oil and seasoning. This mixture has become a popular addition to cole slaw and other salads and as a stuffing for numerous savoury dishes.

see: **cole slaw, felafel, pilaf, salad, tartare**

Burrito

Pronounced
BUREE-TO (with u as in fur, ee as in see and o as in over)

Origin
Burrito is Spanish for a *little donkey.*

Meaning
A **burrito** is a **tortilla**, which is warmed and then filled with a variety of ingredients. It is then rolled into a long cigar shape. A typical filling would be refried beans, grated cheese, chopped tomatoes, shredded lettuce and chilli sauce.

Associations
In Mexico, a **chimichanga** is a deep-fried burrito. Mexican beans are called **frijoles.** There are over 60 varieties used in Mexican cuisine.

see: **tortilla**

Cacciatore

Pronounced
KACHA -TORA (with a's as in far and o as in over)

Origin
Cacciatore is Italian for *hunter or* huntsman from *cacciare* meaning *to go hunting.* When the term **cacciatore** or the French **chausseur** are used, it means that dishes are cooked in the *hunter style, meaning with meat, wine and local, seasonal vegetables.*

chicken cacciatore

Meaning

Chicken **cacciatore** is made with red wine, mushrooms, onions, tomatoes, garlic, olive oil , oregano, seasoning and pieces of chicken.

Associations
see: **casserole, goulash**

Cajan-Creole

Pronounced KAY-JAN (with ay as in say and a as in pan) , KREE - OL (with ee as in see and o as in got)

Origin
The **Cajans** were descendants of French settlers, called originally **Arcadians,** who were forced out of Canada and settled in Lousiana in the Bayon (Riverside) area in the south east of the United States in the 1750's. **Arcadian** was difficult to say for some, so it became **cadian** and then with time the easier **cajan.** The term **creole** derives from the Spanish **criollo** and the French **créole** *a home-born slave.* It was later used to describe

43

the people of French or Spanish stock who lived in Louisiana but whose descendants did not originate there. That is people of local origin. The **Cajan-creole** dishes have evolved from a melange of French, Spanish and American negro cuisines.

Meaning
Cajan-Creole cuisine uses basic foods (vegetables, stewed meats, seafood and rice) and spices, especially peppers (black cayenne), chillies , garlic and tabasco (made from vinegar, red pepper and salt). **Okra** is used extensively, especially for **gumbos**.

Associations
Jambalaya is a spicy, piquant **Cajun-Creole** rice dish. A sauce to accompany the rice is made from onions, capsicum, mushrooms, tomatoes, white wine , hot chillies, garlic and cayenne pepper. It can be served with smoked sausage, chicken breast or prawns and other shellfish.
see: gumbo

Canapé

Pronounced KANAPAY (with a's as in cat and ay as in say)

Origin
Canapé is French for a *sofa.* Canapé then came to mean a slice of bread fried in butter, which is the *"seat"* or *"sofa"* on which small portions of food could *sit.*

Meaning
A **canapé** (which is also called a **croûton** in France) is a piece of toast or fried bread or a savoury biscuit or pastry, made into various interesting shapes, that is covered with a small savoury titbit made from meat, sausage, fish, shellfish, poultry, game, cheese, egg or salad. Often sauces are also part of the savoury addition. They can be presented very simply or be the most elaborate creations. They are served as snacks, savouries, appetizers or hors d' oeuvres.

Associations
Crostini are Italian rustic canapés. The German **häppchen** (meaning *little mouthful*) is a kind of canapé, like a French bouchée.
see: **bouchée, crouton, hors d'oeuvre, tortilla**

Carbonade

Pronounced KAR-BON-AD (with first a as in father, o as in on and final a as in made)

Origin
Carbonnade in French means *grilled meat.* Originally the meat wás grilled over coals called **carbone. Carbonata** in Italian and **Cardinado** in Spanish both meant *cooked over coals.* The meaning has changed, as people nowadays rarely cook over coals. The word has come to mean a **stew** rather than a **grill.**

Meaning
Carbonade (or **carbonnade** in French cuisine) is a Flemish (Belgian) casserole dish. Strips of browned chuck steak, onions, garlic, thyme and bay leaf are simmered in light ale and water in a tightly-closed pan. The beer evaporates but it leaves a sweet

and distinctive flavour to the dish. The top of the casserole is covered with pieces of bread lightly spread with French mustard, which soak up the fat and sauces and are cooked to a golden, crispy brown. A carbonade is often served with dumplings to make a hearty meal.

Associations
see: casserole, dumplings

Cassata

Pronounced KAS-ATA (first a as in cat, second and third a's as in palm)

Origin
Cassata probably originates from the Latin **caseus** meaning cheese. **Cassata** originally referred to a **Sicilian Easter dessert**, which was a sponge cake filled with fresh ricotta cheese flavoured with vanillla. Later cassata referrred to an icecream.
The Ancient Roman emperors were fond of simple iced dishes. Ice cream was invented by the Ancient Chinese and the process of making it was carried to India and Middle East countries. It was probably first brought to Europe by Marco Polo in the 13th century. Icecream, as we know it, where egg yolks and syrups are frozen, was invented in the early 1600's in Italy, especially by two Italians called Pratti and Torteni. It was introduced into Paris, about 1630 by   an Italian, Procopio Coltelli who established the Café Procope, which became very famous.   Dr. Samuel Johnson, the famous English dictionary writer, enjoyed icecream while in France and popularised the dish in England in the mid 18th century.

Meaning
Cassata consists of layers of different flavoured icecreams. Each layer is of a different colour and each is frozen individually and then one is placed on top of another before a final freezing. Chopped crystallised fruit (e.g. cherries, apricots and pineapple) and nuts usually enrich the icecreams and the top of the "cake" is often covered with chocolate. It is served in muli-coloured slices as a snack or dessert.

Associations
see: dessert

Casserole

Pronounced KASA-ROL (with first a as
in cat, second as in ago and o as in over)

Origin
Casserole is derived from the Old French **casse** and the Latin
cattia meaning a *frying pan* or *saucepan*. As has happened often,
the name of a cooking utensil was used for the dish itself.

Meaning
A **casserole** is an ovenproof or flame-proof dish or pan that has
a tight lid. It is used to cook meat and vegetables slowly. Some

beef
casserole

casserole dishes are very attractive and food is sometimes served
at table straight from the casserole dish. A **casserole** is also a
stew or ragoût consisting of meat and vegetables which are put in
a casserole dish at the same time and cooked by stewing. Some
meats are best cooked **en casserole** (as the French say), as the
meat (e.g. rabbit) absorbs the flavours of the vegetables and
spices.

Associations

A **cassoulet** (which was first made in Languedoc in the south west of France) is a casserole which consists of different kinds of meat (usually five kinds) one of which should be pork and another a bird, such as goose, duck or chicken. The dish must also include white haricot beans, sausage and garlic. The dish takes a long time to prepare and cook as each meat should be cooked separately before the complete dish is simmered slowly. A **ghivetch** (which derives from the Turkish word **güvec**, meaning *a cooking pot*) is a casserole of vegetables (e.g. carrots, potatoes, beans, squash, zuchini, onions, cauliflower, peppers, peas, beans, celery) and meat with garlic, which is simmered in a bouillon. A famous Finnish casserole is **Karelian hotpot**, a mixture of meats which is served with rice-filled pasties. In France, **lapin au moutarde** (rabbit with mustard sauce) is a popular casserole, as is the Spanish casserole **picadillo**, which has varied meats and vegetables. A dish which is spectacular when it is served is **pozharsky** (which is Russian for *fire*), which is a Russian meat and vegetable casserole which is set aflame with brandy before it is served. Other well-known casseroles are **Lancashire hotpot** (England), **choesels** (Belgium), **For kal** and **svenska panna** (Sweden) and **Irish stew** (Ireland).

see: **bonne femme, cacciatore, carbonade, coq au vin, croûte, daube, dumpling, feijoada, gumbo, goulash, korma, navarin, osso buco, paella, pilaf, pot au feu, ragoût, ratatouille, salmis, scone**

Cassolette

Pronounced KASO-LET (with a as in fat, o as in over and e as in met)

Origin
Cassolette is French for a *perfume pan* or an *incence burner*. It then came to mean a small dish for food sufficient for one person.

Meaning
A **cassolette** is a small, one-portion dish, which is usually made from earthenware. It is filled with a savoury ragoût, such as ham and chicken with duchess potatoes and topped with grated cheese.

It can also mean a very small case made from fried bread, pastry or egg and bread crumbs which is filled with a savoury mixture. They are served as snacks, appetizers or hors d'oeuvres .

Associations
see: appetizer, barquette, hors d'oeuvre, ramekin, vol au vent

---

Caviar

Pronounced KAV-EEA (with first a as in cat, ee as in see and final a as in far)

Origin
Caviar is from the Persian word **khav-yar** meaning *cake of strength*, because it was thought that caviar had restorative powers and the power to give one long life. The fish from which roe is extracted are caught mainly in the Caspian sea but they

fillet of fish
with caviar
garnish

are also caught in the Gironde Estuary near Bordeaux in Western France.

Meaning
Caviar (also spelled **caviare**) is one of the most expensive foods in the world. This is because it is the salted roe of the female sturgeon fish, which takes up to twenty years to mature before it produces eggs (called **berries**) and because the roe must be extracted from the fish very carefully by hand immediately it has been killed, otherwise the roe hardens and is not edible. **Beluga caviar** with large, light pearl- grey berries is taken from the largest species of sturgeon and is considered the finest caviar. **Osetrova** (or **oscetra**) **caviar** with small pearl-grey to brownish berries is taken from a medium-sized sturgeon and **sevruga caviar** with small almost black berries is taken from the smallest sturgeon and is considered of lower quality than the other two varieties. Caviar is usually served on toast with lemon as a canapé, appetizer or hors d'oeuvre and traditionally is accompanied by champagne or iced vodka.

Associations
Capelin roe and **lumpfish roe** are sold as inexpensive substitutes for caviar.

In Russia, caviar is called **ikra**.

see: appetizer, canapé, hors d'oeuvre

Chapati

Pronounced CHAU-PATEE (with first au as in daub, a as in father and ee as in see)

Origin
Chapati derived from the Hindi **chupatty** meaning a *thin cake of unleavened bread.*

Meaning
A **chapati** is a round, flat unleavened Indian bread (rather like a tortilla or pancake), which is usually made from **roti** (a grainy-textured flour) with salt, ghee and luke-warm water. In India, it is cooked on a saucer-shaped griddle called a **tava** (or **tawa**) and is then often served with a variety of foods on a

personal tray called a **thali**. It is most commonly eaten in North India with curry.

Associations
see: **curry, ghee, tortilla**

Charcuterie

Pronounced SHA-KOOTA-REE (with first a as in father, oo as in moon, second a as in ago and ee as in see)

Origin
Charcuterie is French for *pig meat* or a *pork butcher's meat,* much of which is preserved food. It derived from the French **charcuter** meaning *to cut up into small pieces,* usually fairly roughly. The Ancient Romans discovered and perfected ways of conserving and preparing all the meat from a pig.

Meaning
The term **charcuterie** embodies not only pork but a mixture of pork and game and other meats, such as chipolatas, chorizo, crepinettes, foie gras, galantine, ham and rillettes. When charcuterie is served in a restaurant, one receives a plate of varied meats, such as hams (jambon braisé, cru, blanc, persillé), various slices of sausages and terrines with garnishes.

Associations
see: **chipolata, chorizo, foie gras, galantine, gammon, hors d'oeuvre, rillette, sausage, terrine**

Charlotte

Pronounced SHA -LOT (with a as in father and o as in got)

Origin
Charlotte is a corruption of the Old English word **charlyt** meaning a *dish of custard.* The dessert **charlotte Russe** was invented in the 19th century by the famous French chef -Antonin Carême, during a visit to Russia.

Meaning
One meaning of a **charlotte** is a round mould about 8 to 10 cms deep,with sloping sides so that the inside can be lined with sponge fingers or some other lining without it falling down. Another meaning of the term is a dessert made by lining a mould with sponge fingers, slices of buttered, crustless bread or wafers and then filling the centre with a cream (e.g. **bavarois**) or with cooked sliced fruit (e.g. apple, as in **apple charlotte**) or a fruit purée. **Charlotte Russe** has a lining of savoy fingers and a filling of jelly and bavarian cream and is decorated with cherries and angelica. **Charlotte Malakoff** has a lining of lady fingers and a centre filling of a soufflé concoction of cream, butter, caster sugar, a liqueur, chopped almonds and whipped cream. It is decorated with strawberries. A charlotte should be kept in a refigerator until the last minute before serving.

Associations
see: **bavarois, dessert, purée, soufflé, timbale**

Châteaubriand

Pronounced SHATO-BREEAN (with a as in cat, o as in over , ee as in see and an as in sang nasalised)

Origin
Châteaubriand was invented by Mireil, the chef of François Réne Visconte de Châteaubriand, who was a famous French writer of the early 19th century.

Meaning

A **châteaubriand** is a choice beef steak weighing about 200 to 250 grams, which is cut from the middle (the "eye") of the fillet. It is grilled or sautéed in butter. There is sufficient meat for two people and, traditionally, the fillet is cut at the table, being sliced downwards. It is usually served with maître d'hôtel butter or béarnaise sauce and château potatoes.

Associations

see: **beurre, béarnaise, fillet**

Chaud-froid

Pronounced SHO -FRWA (with o as in over and a as in cat)

chicken chaud-froid

Origin

Chaud is French for *hot* and **froid** for *cold*. The name **chaud-froid** was coined by the Maréchal de Luxembourg at the Château Montmirency in 1759. He was called away from a banquet on urgent business and when he returned late, he ate only one dish, a chicken fricassée in its own sauce, which had gone cold. He enjoyed the dish so much that cooked food presented cold with a sauce became popular at his banquets and at those of others of the aristocracy.

Meaning

A **chaud-froid** is a smooth warm sauce used to coat fish, poultry, game, meat, egg dishes and galatines which are to be served cold with a high-gloss finish. There are several varieties of the sauce. A **white chaud-froid** is made from a base of béchamel or velouté sauce. A **brown chaud-froid**, which is less often served, is made with a base of Espagnole (brown) sauce. Both are seasoned and aspic jelly and a little gelatine are added to ensure the sauce sets when it is cold.

Associations

see: aspic, béchamel, Espagnole, galatine, velouté

Chickpeas

Pronounced CHIK -PEEZ (with i as in pick and ee as in see)

Origin

Chickpeas, one of the oldest cultivated foods in the world, is a native of West Asia and India but is now produced throughout the world. It was first cultivated in Egypt. Remains of cultivated peas found in Switzerland have been carbon dated at 4500 B.C. The word **pease**, the Old English term for *pea*, is of Sanskrit origin. The word **chickpeas** derives from the Latin **cicer**, which in Italian was **cece**.

Meaning

The **chickpea**, of which there are several varieties, is a large dried pea (about 1 to 2 cms in diameter), which can be heart-shaped or round and coloured yellow, pale tan or dark brown. It is a very important ingredient in many dishes from many countries, particularly in North Africa and the Middle East.

It can be cooked and served alone with spices (e.g. in the Greek and Turkish dip called **hummus** or the Mexican dip called **Garbanzo**), added to soups (particularly in Spain) and stews or it can be an accompaniment and garnish to many savoury dishes. Toasted and salted, they make an excellent appetizer or snack (called **chat** in India) and can also be used in salads. Coated with sugar, they are served with tea and coffee in some Middle East countries. Chickpeas are ground to make a fine flour with a very distinctive taste, which is called **besan**. It is used extensively in India and the Middle East .

Associations

The Greeks have a chickpeas soup called **revydia**, which is made from cooked and mashed chickpeas, with chicken broth, onions, olive oil, salt, lemon juice and parsley. The Indian dish **ghana gosth** is lamb or chicken cooked with chickpeas. Very popular in India are **pakoras**, which are spiced vegetables, coated with a chick-pea batter and deep fried. The French for chickpea is **pois chiche** and the Italian is **ceci**.

see: **appetizer, couscous, felafel, salad, tahini**

Chiffonade

Pronounced
SHIF-ONAD (with i as in ship, on as in song nasalised and a as in made)

Origin
Chiffe is the French for a *rag*. **Ade** is a suffix meaning *derived from*. **Chiffonade** was coined to describe something torn into shreds or ribbons .

Meaning
A **chiffonade** is a dish consisting of a mixture of green vegetables, such as spinach, lettuce and sorrel which are shredded or cut finely into ribbons. Sometimes molten butter is added. They form a bed for a dish such as egg mayonnaise or as a garnish for soups.

Associations
see: **mayonnaise, salad**

Chilli

Pronounced CHILY (with i as in pin and y as in duty)

Origin

Chilli is Spanish word for the dried pod or fruit of the **capsicum**, also called a **pepper**, of which there are 140 varieties, some of which are not at all hot and others mouth- blistering ! They are coloured red or green. The **word** chilli originated in what is now Texas, which used to be a part of Mexico. Chillis have always been a very important ingredient in Chinese and Indian cuisines .

Meaning

Chilli is also spelled **chili** and **chile**. The seeds of chillis are the hottest part and they are usually removed and the pods are ground and sieved. Commercial growers of chillis rate chillis for pungency and heat on a scale of 1 to 20. **Green peppers** (also called **bell peppers**) are mild, as are **anahan** or **California**. **Jalapenos** and **serranos** are hot and **chilitepins** and **birds-**

chilli con carne

eye chillis are very hot. Chillis can be used fresh or canned (when they are milder) and are roasted or deep fried. Chilli powders purchased in shops consist not only of ground chillis but also cummin and coriander. Chinese chilli sauce is made from chillis, salt and vinegar and is very hot.

Associations

Chilli con carne, Spanish for *chilli with flesh* (meat), is a well-known chilli dish now eaten throughout the world. **Paprika** is Hungarian red pepper. When red chilli pods are dried and ground, **cayenne pepper** is made. **Pimiento** is the Spanish name for **red capsicum**. It should not be confused with **pimento**, which is another name for **all spice**.

see: **burrito, Cajan-Creole, curry, feijoada, felafel, nasi goreng, sambal, satay, tortilla, vindaloo**

Choux

Pronounced SHOO (with oo as in moon)

Origin

Choux derives from the French word **chou** (plural **choux**) which means *cabbage*. It was used to describe layered pastry, as the layers were thought to resemble the leaves of cabbage!

Meaning

Choux is a kind of pastry made from a smooth dough consisting of plain flour, water, salt, butter, eggs and, if the pastry is to be used for sweet puffs, with sugar. It is mixed in a pan over heat. The pastry is lightened (made more puffy) by steam that builds up in the batter. In France, it is called **pâte à choux**. It is used for **éclairs, profiteroles, beignets, cream puffs, savoury puffs** and **gâteaux**. A **gougère** is a savoury, cheese-flavoured ring or crown of choux pastry. It is made from water, butter, salt, sieved flour, lightly-beaten eggs, seasoning, a pinch of mustard and finely-diced or grated gruyère, which is a hard, pale yellow, tasty, Swiss cheese honeycombed with holes. The ring is made by joining egg-sized pieces of dough in a buttered pie dish or on foil and then by smoothing their tops and the inner circle of the ring. The dish is sprinkled with diced cheese and baked in an oven. The **gougère** is sometimes served with a cheese course or as an appetizer or snack.

Associations
see: beignets, croquemebouche, éclair, gâteau, pâte, gnocchi, profiterole, ramekin

Chowder

chowder

Pronounced CHOWDA (with ow as in now and a as in ago)

Origin

Chowder was first made in Brittany in West France by the wives of fishermen. To welcome their husbands home from the bitterly cold sea, the women prepared a hearty hot fish stew. They cooked the dish in a **chaudière**, from which the term **chowder** derives. The dish is now very popular in New England and the Eastern Seaboard of the United States, where **clam chowder** is a speciality.

Meaning

There are several varieties of **chowder** which are usually made with white fish or shellfish but it is also made with pork and vegetables and with a combination of meat and fish. A fish stock is first produced. To the stock is added fried onions, mashed or sliced potatoes, tomato paste, a little tabasco sauce and curry powder, seasoning and flour to thicken. The mixture is brought to the boil and then slowly simmered. Flaked fish fillets and cleaned shellfish are stirred in and sometimes sliced pickled pork or bacon is included.   The dish is simmered until the fish is cooked and then the chowder is garnished with parsley.

Associations

see: **bisque, bouillabaisse,crustacean, stock**

Coleslaw

Pronounced KOL - SLAW (with o as in over and aw as in saw)

Origin
Coleslaw is derived from the Latin **colis** meaning a *stem*, especially of **cabbage**. In Old English cabbage was called **cal**. It became **kol** (German **kohl**) which became a general term for all kinds of cabbage. **Slaw** is from the Dutch word **slaa** meaning *sliced cabbage* , which is eaten as a salad. The term **coleslaw** is a late 19th century term which originated in the United States.

Meaning
There are many versions of **coleslaw**, which is a salad of raw fruit and fresh,crisp salad vegetables (e.g. celery, cucumber, capsicums, carrots), which always includes **shredded cabbage** and usually grated apple. Sometimes chopped nuts are added. The dish can be tossed lightly in a mayonnaisse or a French dressing. It can be served alone or with ham and other cold meats.

Associations
see: **dressing, mayonaisse, salad**

Compote

Pronounced
KOMPOT (with o's as in got) or KOMPO (with first o as in got and second o as in over)

Origin
Compote derives from the French **composte** which is from **composer** meaning *to put together.* **En compote** in French means *stewed* and the word **compote** means fruits that are *put together* to be stewed .

Meaning
A **compote** consists of fresh and dried fruits (such as apples, apricots, plums, figs and prunes) which are stewed in a flavoured sugar or liqueur syrup and then are served either hot or cold. Sometimes they are sprinkled with kirsch or some other liqueur. The term also describes a stew of birds, such as pigeon and partridge.

Associations

Khosaaf is a Syrian version of a **compote**. The Germans are very fond of stewed fruit, which they call a **kompot**.
see: **dessert, macédoine, salad**

Consommé

Pronounced KON-SOMAY (with o's as in on and ay as in say)

Origin

Consommé is from the Latin **consummare** meaning *to consummate* or *finish perfectly* and *raise to the highest point of achievement.*

Meaning

As the origin indicates, **consommé** is considered one of, if not **the** finest of soups from the 2000 which are served. It is a clear soup and it is essential to use stock made from raw meat which has been clarified by the addition of stiffly-beaten egg white and clean egg shells. To the stock are added onions, celery, carrots and seasoning, a sprig of parsley and a bay leaf and perhaps, a little sherry. The soup is then strained through fine muslin. There are many consommé soups, which are named after either the contents used in them or the garnishes used with them. **Consommé Diane** is made with game. **Consommé Amiral** is made with fish. **Consommé Julienne** includes matchsticks of carrot, turnip and solid savoury custard cut into fancy shapes. **Consommé Madrilene** is a beef consommé with cubes of beef or chicken and vegetables julienne. **Banquet consommé** has vegetables julienne and smoked salmon. **Consommé à la Celestine** is served with cheese pancakes. **Consommé Imperatrice** has chicken, asparagus tips, cocks' combs and kidney. **Consommé frappé** is iced clear soup.

Associations

Kraftbruhe is a clear, aromatic consommé which is popular in Germany. A delicious accompaniment to consommé is the Russian savoury pancake roll or pattie called a **piroshki** or **pirozhki**.
see: **julienne, marmite petite, poularde, stock, velouté**

Coq au vin

Pronounced KOK - O -VA (with first o as in got, second o as in port and a as a nasalised a in sang)

Origin

Coq is French for *cock, rooster* or *chicken.* **Au** means *with* or *in* and **vin** means *wine.* **Coq au vin** means literally *chicken in wine.*

coq au vin

Meaning

Coq au vin is a classic French casserole, which is now popular throughout the world. It consists of pieces of chicken, sautéed button onions, bacon, mushrooms, chopped garlic and a bouquet garni, which are browned in a casserole dish. Any fat is then removed and a little brandy is added to flame the contents, which are then covered with red wine. The casserole is simmered slowly and, if necessary, can be thickened with kneaded butter.

Associations

see: **casserole, poularde**

Coquille St.Jacques

Pronounced KOK-EEYA -SA-ZHAK (with o as in got, ee as in see, y as in yacht, first a as in a in ago but hardly sounded , second a as in ah nasalised, zh as s in measure and final a as in cat)

scallops

Origin

Coquille is French for a *shell* - of a snail, oyster or other shellfish. **Coquillage** is French for *shellfish*. **Coquille St. Jacques** is French for a *scallop* (also spelled *scollop*), which is a bivalve shellfish with a very soft body and a deep shell which is divided into grooves and ridges. The name **St. Jacques** comes from the shrine of **Saint Jacques** (or **James**) of **Compostela** in Spain, which pilgrims visited. The pilgrims used to wear one valve of the shell as a badge to indicate that they had visited a shrine. As the shells of the scallop were deep, they were found to be very useful as plates or dishes. The name of the shell became associated with the name of the shellfish - the **scallop.**

Meaning

Coquilles St. Jacques are cooked in white wine with a little salt, peppercorn, parsley, bay leaf, chopped shallots and water in a saucepan. They are cooked for only about five minutes, otherwise they lose their tenderness. A sauce of fish stock, butter, flour, milk, egg yolks and cream accompanies them.

Associations
See: **crustacean**

Cordon bleu

Pronounced KORDON -BLA (with first o as in morning, second o as in on and a as in a nasalised a as in ago)

Origin
Cordon bleu is French for *blue ribbon* or *cord*. From the time

of Louis XV of France (1710-1774), a blue ribbon was given as an honour to people of the highest distinction. Almost as a joke, it was also bestowed on highly-skilled female cooks, but was later recognised as a mark of distinction in French cuisine.

Meaning

A famous and popular dish is **veal cordon bleu.** A fillet of veal is pounded until it is thin and then it is sliced. Each slice is covered with a piece of ham, which in turn is topped with a slice of gruyère cheese. The bundle is folded in half and dipped into a mixture of flour and eggs and then breadcrumbed and fried in hot butter or oil until a golden brown. It is served with a garnish of fresh vegetables or salad.

cordon bleu with avacado and carrots

Associations

see: **fillet, garnish, scallopini, schnitzel, vitello tonato**

Coulis

Pronounced KOOLEE (with oo as in moon and ee as in see)

Origin

Coulis is French for a *jelly,* made from meat or a *thick sauce.* The word **coulis** (or **cullis**) was generally used in France in the past for a **sauce.**

Meaning

A **coulis** is a concentrated sauce made from the juices which run out of meat when it has been cooked. It also describes a purée of fruit or vegetables, which is not thickened in any way by added ingredients. It can be cooked or uncooked and be hot or cold. It is frequently used as an accompanying sauce. The word **coulis** is also used in some restaurants to mean a thick soup.

Associations
see: **au jus, purée**

Couscous

Pronounced KOOS-KOOS (with oo's as in soon)

Origin
Couscous derives from the Arabic word **kuskus** or the Persian (now Iranian) **khas-khas** meaning *to pound to a small size.* It is a dish consisting of tiny pellets of crushed durum wheat or rice and salted water. The name of the pan or

pot in which the dish was made was called in different parts of North Africa **kuskus, kouskous** and **koskosou.** It is the national dish of Morocco and has been a staple food in all the Middle East countries and North Africa from the earliest times.

Meaning
There are a number of recipes for **couscous,** which vary from one part of the world to another. It always has a base of semolina, made from finely-ground millet flour, which is steamed (three separate times for the best results) in a couscous bowl, cullender or bain marie over boiling water or stock until it is light and quite fluffy. It is served with what is called in Arabic **marga**

meaning *the rest on top.* This is usually a stew of mutton or chicken and vegetables, called in Morocco a **tagine.** The dish is often served with **garbanzos,** a chickpeas sauce.

Associations
The Egyptians call couscous **couscoussi.**
see: bain marie, chickpeas, semolina

Crème -
Anglaise, brûlée, caramel, chantilly, fouettée, fraîche, pâtissière, renversé

Pronounced Crème (KRAIM with ai as in fair), **Anglaise** (AN-GLAZ with first a as in bat, the second as in date), **brûlée** (BROO-LAY with oo as in soon and ay as in say), **caramel** (KARA-MEL with a's as in cat and e as in bell), **chantilly** (SHAN-TEEYAY with a as in band, ee as in see, y as in yes and ay as in say), **fouettée** (FOO-ETAY with oo as in moon, e as in pet

66

and ay as in say), **fraîche**   (FRAYSH with ay as in say), **pâtissiére** (PATEES-YAIR with a as in fat, ee as in see, y as in yes and air as in fair), **renversé** (RON-VAIR-SAY with on as a nasalised on in song, ai as in fair and ay as in say)

Origin & Meaning

Crème derives from the Latin **chrisma** and the Old French **cresme**.

The following words to describe **crèmes** are French. **Crème** means *cream,*

Anglaise means *English.* **Crème Anglaise** is **custard**, which is made from beaten eggs, milk, sugar and some flavouring. It is cooked either over hot water or in an oven.

Brulée means *burnt (caramelised).* **Crème brulée** is also known as **burnt cream** or **Trinity cream**. It is a custard cream topped with a layer of brown sugar which is caramelised under a grill.

Caramel means *caramel (burnt sugar).* **Crème caramel** consists of a vanilla custard which is made in a mould at the

crème caramel

bottom of which is a caramel sauce.

Chantilly means from Chantilly in the Oise area of Northern France. **Crème Chantilly** is lightly-whipped cream which has been sweetened with sugar and flavoured with vanilla. It is used with many cakes and meringues.

Fouettée means *whipped* or *whisked*. **Crème fouettée** is a term in French cuisine for **whipped cream.**

Fraîche means *fresh*. **Crème fraîche** means fresh cream

Pâtissière means a *pastrycook*. **Crème pâtissière** is also called **crème frangipane.** It is a pastry cream made of egg yolks, sugar, flour, vanilla and milk, which is used by pastrycooks for fillings.

Renversé means to turn upside down or invert. **Crème renversé** is French for baked custard, which is used in crème caramel. It is made in a mould which is *turned upside down* when the custard is set onto a serving plate.

Associations

Crème de riz is fine rice flour which is used for thickening sauces. **Ganache** is a cream chocolate, popular in France as a dessert. **Crémet** is a milk curd with egg whites, sugar and cream which is a speciality of the Dauphinois area of France. The Italian **alla panna** means *with cream* .

see : **meringue, mousse, mousseline, pavlova, pikelet, pithiviers, quiche, savarin, schnitzel, soufflé**

Crêpe

Pronounced KRAYP (with ay as in say)

Origin

Crêpe which is French for *pancake* is derived from **creper** meaning *to crisp.*

Meaning

A **crêpe** (or **pancake**) is made from batter comprising beaten eggs, flour, melted butter, a pinch of salt (if desired) and a liquid, such as water or milk or even beer. The batter is poured into a frying pan containing hot oil or butter and fried on both sides until fairly crisp. The pan used for crêpes must be scrupulously clean, as the batter takes the flavour of anything

seafood crêpe

that has been fried previously in the pan. Some people use one pan exclusively for crêpes (and omelettes). Crêpes can be savoury (e.g. filled with ham, mushrooms, cheese, seafood, chopped chicken, asparagus and spinach) or sweet (e.g. filled with fruit, purées or flavoured with a liqueur). Probably the most famous crêpe dish is **crêpe Suzette,** named after Mme Suzette, a star of the Comedie Francaise Theatre in Paris. In a restaurant, a **crêpe Suzette** is often prepared in a chafing dish in full view of the guests. The wafer-thin crêpes are served hot with a sauce of sugar, orange juice and liqueur (usually Grand Marnier). Brandy is poured over the crêpes, lit dramatically and then the crêpes are served when the flames have expired.

Associations

In Spain, pancakes are called **panqecas,** in Germany **pfannkuchen. Dosa** in India are pancakes made from a batter of rice and lentils. **Nalistuki** are crisp Russian crêpes filled with cheese and **lingon pannkakor** are Swedish crêpes filled with lingonberries. **Palacsinta** are very thin Hungarian crêpes, which are served as a dessert or with soups. **Clafouti** is a thick fruit pancake in France, which is usually made with stoned, black cherries in a batter which is cooked in a flan case.

Croissant

Pronounced KRWA-SON with a as in cat and on like a naselised on in song

Origin

Croissant is French for *crescent-shaped* - like the waxing moon. The word **croissant** as a food originated when the Turks were besieging Budapest, the capital of Hungary, in 1686. Bakers working late at night heard the Turks tunneling to get into the fortified city. They gave the alarm and the Turks were repelled. The bakers were honoured by being allowed to bake a special pastry in the shape of a crescent, the emblem on the Turkish flag.

Meaning

A **croissant** is a crescent-shaped roll of flaky pastry. It is very popular in France, and increasingly in other countries, as part of breakfast. It is usually served with **confiture** (French for *jam*) or butter. Croissants filled with a tasty, savoury filling are also served as snacks, appetizers or hors d'oeuvres.

Associations

Kab el ghzail are North African almond croissants.
see: **appetizer, hors d'oeuvre, pomme**

Croquembouche

Pronounced KROK-ON -BOOSH (with o as in lock, on as a nasalised on in song, oo as in soon)

Origin

Croquembouche derives from the French **croquer** meaning *to munch* or *crunch*, **em** is an old form of **en** meaning *in* and **bouche** means *mouth*. Croquembouche literally means *crunch in the mouth*.

Meaning

A **croquembouche** consists of balls of baked choux pastry (like profiteroles) or of meringue. They are stacked in a pyramid or cone shape with a space in the middle, which is filled with chantilly or some other cream. Cones on which the choux puffs can be assembled can be purchased. The pastry is covered with a lace of spun, caramelised sugar. It is the traditional French "wedding cake". At Christmas in France, it is decorated with angelica and cherries or caramelised fruits, such as orange segments dipped in toffee.

Associations

see: choux, crème, meringue, profiteroles

Croquette

Pronounced KRO-KET (with o as in got and e as in pet)

Origin

Croquette is derived from the French **croquer** meaning to *crunch* or *munch*. **Ette** is a suffix meaning *small*. It means literally, *a small crunchy morsel*.

Meaning

Croquettes come in various shapes : balls, pear-shaped and barrel-shaped. They are made from a wide variety of ingredients, such as minced meat, fish or poultry, mashed potatoes, rice, tapioca and semolina. The main ingredient is bound with egg yolk or a mixture of butter, egg, flour and milk. Seasoning is added and the croquette is shaped and then dipped in egg and breadcrumbs. It is fried in hot oil in a frying basket until golden brown and crispy.

Associations

The Italian croquette, called a **crochette,** has its main ingredient bound with béchamel sauce. In Italy, **suppli al telefono** (literally *croquettes on the telephone*) are cheese-filled balls of rice which are fried in oil. They get their name because when they are broken open, strings of cheese, like telephone wires, come out. In Poland croquettes are called **kromeskies.**
see: **panada, rechauffé, rissole, semolina, tartare**

Croustade

Pronounced KROO-STAD (with oo as in moon and a as in ale)

Origin
Croustade is French for a *pie* or *pasty*

Meaning

A **croustade** is a dish made with puff pastry or flaky pastry which is filled with a savoury filling. It can also consist of a bread roll or small loaf which is hollowed out, brushed with beaten egg and then deep fried. It is then filled with a savoury preparation. The filling is eaten but the croustade may or may not be eaten, according to one's taste. It is served as an appetizer, hors d'oeuvre or entrée.

Associations
see: **appetizer, feuilletage , hors d'oeuvre**

Croûte

Pronounced KROOT (with oo as in moon)

Origin
Croûte is French for *crust , such as* of bread or cheese .

Meaning
A **croûte** is a round or finger of toasted or fried bread about 1 cm thick. Savouries, such as sausage or ham or seafood are served on it, as a snack, appetizer or hors d 'oeuvre. Croûtes which are served as a garnish for casserole dishes or soups are called **croûtons.**

Associations
The Italian for a croûton is **crostino**
see: **appetizer, beef bourguinonne, garnish, hors d' oeuvre, noisette, pâté, pipérade, rillette, salmis, tournedos**

Crudité

Pronounced KROO -DEE -TAY (with oo as in soon, ee as in see and ay as in say)

Origin
Crudité is a French word which derives from the Latin **crudus** and the French **cru** meaning *raw* or *uncooked.*

Meaning
Crudités are raw vegetables or fruit. Vegetables such as carrot, radishes, celery and mushrooms are sliced and cauliflower and broccli are broken into pieces, so that they can be easily handled. The vegetables are arranged on a plate as a separate dish, such as an entrée or appetizer, or become part of a dip, such as **aïoli** or **bagna cauda**.

Associations
see: aïoli , bagna cauda, appetizer, entrée

Crustacean

Pronounced KRUST-ASHAN ('with u as in dust, first a as in late and final as in ago)

Origin
Crustacean derives from the Latin **crusta** meaning *crust, shell* or *hard surface.* **Cean** is a Latin suffix indicating *belonging to.* The word came to mean a class of animals, mainly sea animals, with hard shells. Shellfish were once the food of the very poor. Nowadays, it is almost the opposite.

Meaning

Crustacea (the plural of **crustacean**) refers **in cuisine** to all the edible shellfish with shells, such as **crayfish** (called **crawfish** in the U.S.A.), **lobster** (The **rock lobster** is called a **langoustine** in France.), **mussels** (called **moules** in French dishes), **scallops, scampi** (also called **Dublin Bay prawns**), and **shrimps.** They are used in many seafood soups, salads and as separate main courses. To be precise, octopus, squid, mussels, oysters and clams are **moluscs** rather than **crustacea** but this distinction is rarely made in cuisine.

Associations

Popular oyster dishes are: **oysters Bordelaise**, which are oysters in the half shell, flavoured with seasoning, finely-chopped shallots, and red wine. They are gratinéed in an oven. **Oysters Mornay** are Covered with a mornay sauce and then sprinkled with grated cheese and gratinéed; **oysters Rockefeller** are served with a mixture of finely-chopped cooked spinach and onion, then topped with grated cheese or breadcrumbs and gratinéed; **oysters Kilpatrick** are served with a drop of Worcester

oysters naturel

sauce and seasoning and are covered with a little bacon, which is grilled until crisp. **To shuck** is to remove the shell from a crustacean in order to obtain the meat inside the shell.

see: bisque, bouillabaisse, chowder, coquille St Jacques, gratinée, mornay sauce, paella, pilaf, rissoto, tempura

---

Cuisine

Pronounced   KWI-ZEEN (with i as in pin and ee as in seen)

Origin

Cuisine derives from the Latin **coquina** meaning *cooking* from **coquere** meaning *to cook*. From this term, the French word

cuisiner originated meaning *to cook* and **cuisine** meaning a *kitchen*. In French, a **cuisinier** means a *cook*, a *cookery book* and a *cooking stove*.

Meaning

The word cuisine has come to mean *the art of cooking* or *cookery* both in France and in other countries throughout the world. **Haute cuisine (haute** is French for *high*), which is also called classic or grande cuisine, is a term which has been applied to the cuisine which flourished in the palaces and castles of pre-revolutionary France, through chefs such as Antonin Carême (1784-1833)　and then carried into the early 20th century with Auguste Escoffier (1847 -1935). Elegance of presentation is an essential aspect of haute cuisine. The term has been applied to cuisines other than French, such as　Chinese. The French themselves do not use the term. Nowadays, haute cuisine means food which is recognised as of the highest standard, which is intricately prepared, beautifully decorated and served with grace. **Cuisine naturelle** was a movement in the 1970's and 1980's which emphasised natural products in all dishes. It avoided the use of cream, butter, oil, fat and lard and used very little sugar. **Nouvelle Cuisine**, or as it was first called **La Nouvelle Cuisine Française** (literally the *new French cooking)*, was started by two French chefs, Gault and Millau, in 1974. Like **Cuisine Naturelle**, it avoided rich, flour-thickened sauces in favour of reduced stocks and it placed　strong emphasis on ingredient freshness, lightness of texture, clear favours, simplicity and aesthetic presentation. It　also liked to include fruit with savoury dishes.

Associations

Related to cuisine is the term **culinary**, which derives from　the Latin **culina** meaning a *kitchen*. **Culinary** means anything to do with　*cooking.* In France, a **batterie de cuisine** means the essential kitchen equipment, such as pots and pans and **cuisine bourgeoise** means *plain cooking.*
see: **degustation, pièce de rèsistance, restaurant, sûpreme**

Curry

Pronounced   KURY (with u as in uncle and y as in duty)

Origin
Curry derives from the Tamil (Indian) word **kari** meaning a *seasoned sauce* or *relish*. It originated in the South of India. Turmeric, an East Indian plant of the ginger family, in powder form is an essential ingredient of all curries.

Meaning
Curry is a combination of spices which are added to dishes of meat, poultry fish and vegetables to produce a dish which is also called curry or curried, as in curried chicken or curried lamb. **Curry powder** is generally bought from a grocer's shop and may consist of a blend of about 15 to 20 spices. It should have a mixture of at least 6 spices, such as cardamon, cloves, coriander, cumin, fenugreek, ginger, mace, pepper and turmeric and will

beef curry and accompaniments

usually include chilli powder. In India or Indonesia, however, many cooks prefer to blend their own curries and buy separate spices, which they roast and grind and then add separately to dishes to produce the exact flavours they want. The art of curry making is in the delicate and subtle blending of the flavours of the different spices. Some Indian curries use as many as 40 different spices. The hotness of a curry is largely determined by the amount and kind of chilli used in a blend. North Indian and Pakistan curries are milder than those in the South of India. Madras curries are noted for their hotness. Condiments which may accompany curry dishes are: dried banana flakes, bombay duck, chives, chutneys, dried fruit, ginger, hard-boiled eggs, mandarin oranges, marinated vegetables, nuts (e.g. almonds, cashew, peanuts), onions, peppers, pickles, pimientos, poppadums, raisins, sambals, sour cream and sultanas .

Associations
In South East Asia, curry is called **kares** or **gulehs** and the mixture for curry is called a **garam masala**. In Indonesia, grated or dessicated coconut is a traditional ingredient in curry dishes. Curry is almost always accompanied by rice or bread. A **puris** is a deep-fried, round, wholemeal disc of bread. The pieces of puris dough are fried in hot oil until they swell and are golden brown. They are served with **dry curries**, such as **potato curry**.
see: chilli, chowder, garam masala, kedgeree, mulligatawny, poppadum, rice, vindaloo

---

Dahl

Pronounced   DAL (with a as in father)

Origin
Dhal is a Hindi (Indian) word for a salmon-coloured *split pea* or *lentil* , which is yellow when cooked. It was one of the first crops ever to be cultivated and probably has the longest history of all human foods. It is a staple in the diet of people in India and the Middle East. In Third world countries, it is called "poor man's meat".

Meaning

Dahl (which is also spelled **dal** and **dhal**) is a thick or thin purée of lentils, of which there are many varieties (e.g. **urad, tur, touvar, chana** and **mung dal**). The lentils are boiled and seasoned and spiced to make a soup, a porridge or a dip. It accompanies many Indian and Middle East dishes and is extensively used in Mexico, Turkey and Greece.

Associations
see: **kedgeree, pappadum, rissole, tahini**

Dashi

Pronounced DASHEE(with a as in cat and ee as in see)

Wipe the *konbu* with a damp cloth and cut into 4 pieces with scissors to allow flavor to escape.

Put 4 cups of water and *konbu* into pan and bring to boil over medium heat.

Immediately when water begins to boil, take out *konbu*. Do not overcook.

Add ¼ cup cold water to stop the boiling.

Add 1 cup *katsuobushi* all at once. When water boils again, turn off heat.

When *katsuobushi* has all sunk to the bottom, strain soup through cheesecloth-lined sieve or ordinary fine sieve.

preparing dashi

Photograph from " Japanese Cooking for Health and Fitness" by Kyoko Konishi, published by Gakken & Co. Ltd.

Origin & Meaning

Dashi is Japanese for a *stock*. There are three kinds of **dashi** used in Japanese cuisine. One is **katsuo-dashi**, which is a stock made from flakes of dried **bonito** (called in Japanese **katsuobushi**, pronounced *kats -aw- bush-ee*). **Bonito**, which is called **striped tunny** in Europe, is a fish which belongs to the mackerel family. The second dashi is **konbu-dashi**, which is a stock made from a dried kelp seaweed called **konbu** (pronounced *kon-boo)*. The third is **niboshi-dashi**, which is a stock made from small, dried sardines or anchovies. Dashi is served as a soup or dip in Japan and is also an important stock for other dishes, such as **miso** and **tempura**. It is also used to flavour rice in such a dish as **sushi**.

Associations
see: bouillon, miso, seaweed, stock, sushi, tempura

Daube

Pronounced DOB (with o as in over)

Origin
Daube is from the French **dauber** meaning *to stew* or *braise* and from **daubière** meaning a strong *stewing* or *braising pan with handles.*

Meaning
A **daube** is a hearty beef or mutton stew or casserole. It consists of cubes of beef or mutton which are left overnight to marinate in a marinade of red wine, garlic and herbs. The meat is then layered in a pan (a **daubiére**) with bacon, mirepoix and some marinade. It is then stewed gently and slowly for up to three hours. It is served with a garnish of mushrooms, tomatoes and olives. A well-known French beef daube is **daube de boeuf Provençale**, and a mutton one is **daube de mouton à l'Avigonnaise**.

Associations
see: casserole, garnish, marinade, mirepoix

Dégustation

Pronounced DAY-GOO-STAS-YON (with ay as in day, oo as in moon, a as in cat, y as in yet and on as a nasalised on in song)

Origin
Déguster is French for *to taste* or *to sample*. **Degustation** means a tasting or sampling of food or wine.

Meaning

Dégustation is part of a menu in some restaurants. It is offered as a choice, so that some diners may sample small portions of the entire range of specialities which the chef of the restaurant has to offer. It is thought that in this way a diner is able to appreciate fully the chef's culinary skill and artistry.

Associations

see: **cuisine, restaurant**

Dessert

Pronounced   DI-ZURT   (with i as in fit and u as in fur)

Origin

Dessert is from the French **desservir** meaning *to clear the table.* In the 18th century, fruit and confections were served after the main meal had been cleared away. Entertainments were usually provided in rich households during the time desserts were served. It was in Arab countries that desserts were first served. The Arabs loved to finish a meal with sweet things. The word **candy** is from the Arabic word for *sugar* .

Meaning

Dessert refers to the sweet course or the last course of a formal meal. Each country has its own specialities for desserts. The term **entremets** (literally meaning *between dishes*) is used in France for the sweet course, as well as the term dessert.

Associations

see: **baba, bavarois, beignet, blanc mange, cassata, charlotte, crême, crêpe, filo, flummery, fool, gâteau, gelato, granite, marron, marzipan, meringue, mousse, parfait, pavlova, pêch melba, rice, salad** savarin, semolina, soufflé, strudel, sundae, tart, torte, trifle, truffle, yoghurt, zabaglione

---

Dim sum

Pronounced DIM SUM (with i as in it and u as in rub)

Origin
Dim sum is Cantonese for *touch the heart,* suggesting that they are pleasurable. They are also called **tim sam** and **Dian xin or dim sim** in Mandarin. They have been part of Cantonese cuisine for hundreds of years.

Meaning
Dim sum are Cantonese dumplings which are steamed in bamboo steamers and then served in them. The dim sum are filled with various savoury fillings made from chicken, seafoods and vegetables or with sweet pastes and preserves. **Dim sum** are part of a very large variety of dishes which are wheeled around on trolleys in Chinese restaurants, for diners to help themselves to their choice of dishes. They can be a snack, an hors d'oeuvre or make a main meal.

Associations
See: dumplings, hors d'oeuvre

Dolmades

Pronounced DOL-MATHES (with o as in on, a as in far and e as in pet)

Origin
Dolmades derives from the Turkish word **dolma** which means *stuffed* or *any stuffed food.* Stuffed vegetables as a culinary innovation began in the Ottoman Empire, which was founded by Othman in the 13th century. They have been called **dolma** or

tolma in the area which is now called the U.S.S.R. for hundreds of years, where they are very popular.

Meaning

Dolmade (or **dolmas**) describes vine leaves or cabbage leaves which are stuffed with minced lamb or with rice, currants and pine nuts and then cooked in a stock. They are served with tomato sauce.

Nowadays, dolmade also describes a cooked food which is presented in the shape of a cigar.

Associations

Dolma also describes an onion stuffed with rice and meat and also courgettes and carrots which are stuffed with a savoury filling . Stuffed vegetables are very popular in Mediterranean and Middle East countries and throughout Russia (the U.S.S.R). The Turks and the Greeks love to eat **dolmadakia**, which literally means *little stuffed things.*

Dressing

Pronounced   DRESING (with e as in press and ing as in sing)

Origin

Dressing derives from the French **dresser** meaning *to prepare* or *to arrange* . One of its meanings in English came to mean to prepare or arrange food ready for eating, especially with a sauce. The French for dressing is **assaisonnement**, meaning a *seasoning* , *relish* and *flavouring.*

Meaning

Dressing in cuisine has two meanings. One is the process of trimming or trussing some foods before they are cooked by removing bits that cannot be, or will not be, eaten (such as fish fins, or inedible parts of vegetables) or by tying so that they are neat for cooking and presentation. It means also a sauce or cream which accompanies vegetables or salads. There are 4 basic dressings of the latter kind: **vinaigrette, mayonnaise, acidulated creams** and **Scandanavian sweet-sour.** Vinegar is common to almost all dressings and this is not only for the flavour it gives but also because it softens the tissues of plants to make them more digestible. **Vinaigrette** is a French oil and vinegar salad dressing consisting of best quality oil (e.g. olive oil), vinegar, a little salt and ground pepper. It has a tangy flavour and a pungent odour. Salad should be dried off before vinaigrette dressing is applied, as surfaces that are wet will repel the oil in the dressing. A vinaigrette dressing, which is one of the best known and most-used dressings, is also known as a **French dressing.** It is said that to produce a perfect French dressing for salad, one should be a spendthrift in the use of oil, a miser in the use of vinegar (usually 3 parts oil to 1 part vinegar) and the most energetic person imaginable in the mixing. Some well-known and popular dressings for salads are: **Russian salad dressing** consisting of mayonnaise and chilli sauce or chopped beetroot and horseradish sauce; **roquefort dressing** consisting of mayonnaise with roquefort cheese; a **thousand islands dressing** consisting of mayonnaise with chilli sauce, chopped green and red peppers and chopped chives; **chatelaine dressing** consisting of equal parts of mayonnaise and cream and **chiffonade dressing** consisting of vinaigrette, chopped, hard-boiled eggs, parsley and chopped beetroot.

Associations
In many countries, **yoghurt**, with accompanying herbs and spices. is used as a dressing for many dishes.
see: **cole slaw, mayonnaise, salad, yoghurt, sashimi**

Dumpling

Pronounced
DUM-PLING (with u as in plum and i as in sing)

Origin
Dumpling derives from the Old English **dump** meaning a short, thick piece of something or from Old German **dump** meaning *something moist*. **Ling** is a suffix meaning *small*. The two meanings were probably combined to describe the thick lump of dough used to make the dish **dumpling**, which came out of the cooking pan moist.

Meaning

Dumplings are made from a dough consisting of flour, water and seasoning (called **pâte à dumpling** in France). They are light and appetizing, if they are steamed in a closed container over water or stock - and not boiled. If they are added to a casserole, it should be at the last minute with just enough time for them to cook. Dumplings can be plain, made with a savoury or sweet addition to the dough or have a savoury or sweet filling.

caramel dumplings

Associations

In Bavaria in Germany, **kartoffelklösse** (*potato dumplings*) and **spätzle** (meaning "*little sparrow* ", which are tiny dumplings) are very popular. Suet dumplings accompany boiled beef in England and in Italy **budino** or **gnocchi** are dumplings which go with a number of dishes. Russians love dumplings which they call **varenyky**. In China, **gow gees** (*fried pork dumplings*) and **shau mai** (*steamed pork dumplings*) are eaten in most parts of the country.
see: casserole, dim sum, gnocchi, quenelle, scone

Duxelle

Pronounced DUX-EL (with u as in uncle and e as in bell)

Origin
Duxelle was named in the 17th century after the Marquis d'Uxelles in France , whose chef, La Varenne, produced the dish.

Meaning
A **duxelle** consists of finely-chopped and seasoned onions and mushrooms. They are fried slowly until they are reduced to a brown, thick mixture. The mixture is used as a garnish (e.g with fish, game or poultry) or as a stuffing for mushrooms or tomatoes. **Sauce duxelle** consists of chopped mushrooms, shallots, butter and wine which are fried to a brown mixture. To this is added tomato paste, chopped herbs, and seasoning. The mixture is served with grilled or roast meat.

Associations
see: **garnish**

Éclair

Pronounced EKLAIR (with e as in get and ai as in fair)

Origin
Éclair is French for *a flash of lightning,* which lasts only momentarily. The choux pastry called an éclair is so light and airy that it lasts in the eating only a very short time.

Meaning
An **éclair** is a cigar-shaped, crisp choux pastry, about 7 to 8 cms long, which is filled with custard cream, fresh cream or pastry cream flavoured with vanilla essence, chocolate or coffee. It is often iced with fondant icing or covered with chocolate or mocha.

Associations
French pastry cream (crème pâtissiére) is often used as a filling in éclairs. It is custard made from eggs, milk and flavouring. It is also known as **confectioner's custard.**
see: **choux, crème, dessert, feuilletage**

Entrecôte

Pronounced ONTRA -KOT (with on as in song but nasalised, a as in ago and o as in over)

Origin
Entre is French for *between* and **côte** means the *side* or *rib.* **Entrecôtes** means literally *between the ribs.*

Meaning
An **entrecôte** is a steak of beef of about 100 to 150 grams, which is cut from between the animal's ribs. The steak is often thinned by pounding it between sheets of oiled paper. It is then grilled or sautéed in butter for about a minute. It is sometimes called a **minute steak.** It can be served with various garnishes.

Associations
see: **fillet**

Entrée

Pronounced   ON-TRAY (with on as in song nasalised and
ay as in say)

Origin
Entrée is French for *entry, entrance* or *beginning.*

avacado and prawns

Meaning
One would think that the **entrée** course would be the first course
of a meal but in formal dinners it is the second course, after the
soup. It consists of some hot or cold, dressed savoury dish of
meat, poultry, game, fish, eggs or vegetables, served with a
garnish. The portions served are always much smaller than those
for a main course. In the U.S.A., an entrée can refer to a main
course or any "*made up* " dish with a sauce.

Associations
**see: barquette, crudité, escargot, foie gras, hors
d'oeuvre, gougère, moussaka, pizza, terrine, vol au
vent, wurst**

Epicure

Pronounced   EPY-KUR (with e as in pet, y as in duty and u
as in cure)

Origin& Meaning

The term **epicure** originated with the Ancient Greek philosopher **Epikoinos**, which was **Epicurus** in Latin. His teachings stated that pleasure and pain are the chief good and evil. It came to mean, however, a person whose main aim in life is pleasure. Nowadays, it means a person who has sensitive and discriminating tastes in food and wine.

Associations

The French call an **epicurean** a **fine bouche** (literally a *discriminating* or *choice mouth*)

see: **gourmet**

Escargot

Pronounced

ES-KAR-GO (with e as in west, a as in father and o as in over)

Origin

Escargot is French for an edible, vineyard snail. Snails were much enjoyed by the Ancient Romans, who farmed them in special pens, similar to the parks **(parc à escargot)** used in France today.

Meaning

Escargot, which are usually an entrée, are served with a sauce made from melted butter, finely-chopped shallots, chopped parsley and garlic which has been pounded to a paste. The mixture is seasoned with salt and pepper and poured when hot into the escargot shell. They are eaten alone or with crusty bread.

Associations

The Italians also breed and eat snails. Their word for the mollusc is **lumache**.

see: **entrée**

Espagnole Sauce

Pronounced ESPA-YOL (with e as in egg, a as in spar and o as in not)

Origin
Espagnole is French for *Spanish* or *Spaniard.* The sauce was called Spanish originally because of its dark appearance.

Meaning
Espagnole sauce is one of the four basic sauces from which all other sauces (and there are hundreds of them) are derived. It is what the French call a **sauce mère** (*mother sauce*). It is a basic **brown sauce**, consisting of brown stock (from meat bones), a brown roux, flour, vegetables and herbs, which is simmered for several hours, then strained until it is reduced. Some recipes include some chopped smoked ham or bacon and mushrooms. Some sauces made with a basis of **sauce Espagnole** are: bigarade, bordelaise, chasseur, creole, diable, madeira and réforme.

Associations
see: **bigarade, bordelaise, chaud-froid, stock**

Feijoada

Pronounced FAY-ZHWA-DA (with ay as in say, zh as s in pleasure, a's as in father)

Origin
In 1819, a Spanish naturalist named J. da Silva Feijoa discovered in Brazil a previously unknown and unnamed tree. He named it the **feijoa tree.** It had a guava-like fruit which was used in a dish, which eventually became the national dish of Brazil - **feijoada.**

Meaning
Feijoada has four parts: meat (including sausage, beef tongue, pigs' feet, spareribs, chuck beef and bacon or ham), rice, black beans or kidney beans and fruit, especially oranges.

Traditionally on festive occasions, the dish has 15 meats! The four parts are cooked separately and then combined for the finished casserole dish. The ingredients vary from one part of South America to another but traditionally the dish comprises dried, salted beef, pork chops, bacon, sausage (e.g. chorizo), garlic, long-grained rice, black beans, banana, tabasco-soaked onion rings, tomatoes, orange slices and chilli. The result is a very hearty and filling dish.

Associations
see: **casserole, chilli, rice, saucisson**

Felafel

Pronounced
FEL-AFEL (with e's as in pet and a as in father)

Origin
Felafel derives from the Arabic **falafil** meaning a *flat bread* which was rolled and stuffed with seasoned vegetables. It has been part of the staple diet of countries in the Middle East for centuries.

Meaning
Felafel (also spelled **filafil**) consists of minced chickpeas, broadbeans, diced onions, lemon juice, crushed wheat flour (**burghul**) or **tahini** and spices. The mixture is made into small balls (like rissoles) or fritters, sprinkled with sesame seeds and deep fried. Felafels are excellent as a hot hors d'oeuvre or as a main dish served with a yoghurt sauce or with a chilli sauce.

Associations
In Israel, felafels are called **Israeli hotdogs**.
see: **burghul, hors d'oeuvre, rissole, tahini, yoghurt**

Fettucine

Pronounced FETA-CHEENAY (with e as in pet, a as in ago, ee as in see and ay as in say)

Origin
Fettucine is Italian for *strips* or *ribbons*. The word describes strips of pasta, which vary in their widths. This shape of pasta originated in Rome and its surrounding area. It is called **tagliatelle** (pronounced TAG-LEE-A-TELLAY) in the north of Italy.

Meaning
Fettucine is one of the most popular of Italian pastas. The strips of pasta are boiled in slightly salted water (with a little oil added to prevent the pasta sticking together) until the pasta is *al dente*. It can be served simply as **fettucine all' Alfredo** with butter and parmesan cheese or with more elaborate meat sauces.

Associations
see: **al and alla (al dente), pasta, parmigiano**

Feuilletage

Pronounced FUR -YA-TAZH (with u as in fur, first a as in cat, last as in father and zh as s in pleasure)

Origin

In French, **feuille** means a *leaf*. **Feuilletage** is derived from feuille and means either *flaky, puff pastry* (which has several leaves) or *the rolling and re-rolling of dough for puff pastry.* Several suggestions have been made about the origin of the process but none is conclusive. What is known for certain from historical records is that flaky pastry was made in Ancient Greece and that it was well known throughout Europe in the 11th century.

Meaning

Flaky or puff pastry, **pâte à feuilletage** or **feuilleté**, as it is called in French cuisine, is the most delicate of all pastries. It is made from dough consisting of sieved flour, water and a little salt. The dough is rolled into sheets and kneaded; shortening (e.g. butter) is placed on the dough which is then folded over the shortening. The dough is rolled and turned six times, producing 1459 layers which spreads the shortening evenly in the dough. During the preparation of the dough, it should be kept cold and should be refrigerated between rolls. When the dough is heated the shortening swells and steam is generated which fills and swells and puffs up the many layers. It can now be readily purchased from shops ready for use. **Feuilletage** is used for pies, patties, tarts, gâteaux, puffs, pastry cases, slices etc.

vol au vent

Associations

In France, **pâte feuilletée** means *puff pastry* and **feuilleté** is a *puff pastry case*. **Feuillatines** are strips of flaky pastry, sprinkled with granulated sugar. They are served with tea or coffee or instead of wafers with ice cream. **Allumettes** are rectangles of puff pastry with a sweet or savoury filling. **Jalousies** are little cakes made of flaky pastry. A **galette**, a flat, round cake, which is the symbolic cake eaten on Twelfth Night in France, is made from flaky pastry. **Bstila**, a Moroccan pie, has 104 layers of flaky pastry stuffed with scrambled eggs and chopped meat from pigeons. A **turnover** is a semi-circular patty or pie of flaky pastry with crumpled edges, which is filled with a **sweet** or savoury filling.

see: **beef Wellington, croustade, filo, gâteau, mille feuille, pithiviers, profiterole, vol au vent**

Feuilleton

Pronounced   FUR-YA-TON (with u as in fur, a as in ago and on as a nasalised on in song)

Origin
Feuilleton is derived from the French **feuillet** meaning the *leaf of a book*. The word was used in cuisine to describe slices of meat which were placed on top of each other, like the leaves of a book.

Meaning
A **feuilleton** is made from thin, flat, rectangular slices of veal or pork, which are spread with a layer of stuffing, seasoned and then laid on top of each other. The mound of meat is then tied and wrapped in a caul or in thin slices of pork fat. It is then braised in stock or wine with onions and carrots.

Fillet

Pronounced   FIL-ET (with i as in pin and e as in naked)

Origin
Fillet is from the Latin **filum** meaning a *thread* or a *thin*

narrow strip of anything. One of its meanings became a strip of meat or fish.

Meaning
A **fillet** is the very tender undercut of beef (e.g **sirloin**), veal or pork. It refers, too, to the boned breast of poultry and winged game and to the boned sides of fish. **To fillet** is to bone something. From the whole fillet pieces may be cut. The smaller end of a beef fillet is used for making **tournedos** and **filet mignon**. **Filet** is French for *fillet* and **mignon** for *dainty, delicate* and *favourite*. A **filet mignon** is traditionally trimmed into the shape of a triangle. It is usually grilled (braised) or sautéed in butter.

a fillet

a delice

Associations
In French **aiguillette** (from the French **aiguille** meaning a **needle**) means *a strip or slice of flesh cut lengthewise, especially of fowl, such as duck.* In France, **grenadin** is a larded veal fillet and **délice** describes a neatly-folded fillet of fish. A **goujon** is a fillet of fish which has been cut into strips then dipped in beaten egg and rolled in breadcrumbs before being deep fried. It is served with a mayonnaise sauce.

paupiettes- fillets, which are stuffed with fish or vegetables then rolled into a barrel shape and tied.

goujons cut into strips

Fileto is the Italian for *fillet.* In the U.S.A., a fillet is called a **tenderloin**.
see: **boeuf Stroganoff, chateaubriand, mayonnaise, noisette, paupiette, quiche, rollmop, saltimboca, sukiyaki, sûpreme, vitello tonnato, tournedos**

fillets of pork with figs

Filo

Pronounced   FEE-LO (with ee as in see and o as in over)

Origin
Filo is from the Greek **phyllon** meaning a *leaf*. The filo baking
process originated in Turkey during the Ottoman Empire, which

was founded by Othman the First (1259-1326)

Meaning

Filo (also spelled **fillo** and **phyllo**) describes paper-thin leaves of pastry dough. It can be made or bought fresh or frozen from many shops. One of the most popular dishes in Greece is **spanikopita**, which consists of filo pastry cases filled with cooked spinach and grated cheese. Another Greek dish, **baklava**, is a dessert made from filo pastry. Each layer of pastry is brushed with melted butter and topped with chopped almonds or walnuts, cinammon and lemon juice It is baked then soaked in a hot sugar syrup or honey. It is then cut into diamond or square shapes and served cold as a dessert or snack. **Seafood bonbons** are made from filo pastry packages filled with seafood.

Associations

see: **appetizer, dessert, feuitellage, spanikopita, strudel**

filo savoury parcel

Flan

fruit flan

Pronounced   FLAN (with a as in pan)

Origin
The **flan** has been part of the cuisine of many countries for over two thousand years. The term originated in cooking from metal work , where a **flan** was a *metal disc*. It was called a flan in cuisine as the metal pastry case resembled   a disc.

Meaning
A **flan** is an open, short-crust pastry which lines a flan case. It is usually baked blind (empty) for filling later with a sweet or savoury   mixture.

Associations
In the U.S.A., a **flan** is known as a **tart** or a **pie**.
see: pizza, quiche, ramekin, tart

Fleuron

Pronounced FLUR-ON (with u as in fur and on as a nasalised on in song)

Origin
Fleuron is French for a *small flower* or a *floral ornament.*

Meaning
Fleurons are small, flower-shaped, oval, diamond, half-moon or crescent-shaped pieces of puff pastry which are usually used as a garnish or decoration on some dishes. They are also used to decorate the tops of pastry crusts or pâtés.

Associations
see: **garnish, pâté**

Florentine

Pronounced FLO-REN-TIN (with o as in got, e as in pen and i as in fine)

Origin
Florentine is a word which describes the city of **Florence** in North Italy. Cooks from Florence are said to have introduced spinach into the French diet in the 16th century.

Meaning
The French call any dish which includes spinach **florentine.** For the Italians, florentine means much more, as it includes the different dishes and ways of cooking of Florence and its surrounding areas. **À la Florentine** describes a garnish of spinach for eggs, sweetbreads and fish. It is usually topped with a mornay sauce. **Eggs florentine** consists of spinach, cream, seasoning, eggs, cheese (gruyère or ementhal) and olives, with paprika optional. The word **florentine** also describes a biscuit which contains nuts and dried fruit. The biscuit's top is covered with chocolate which is decorated with distinctive wavy lines.

Flummery

Pronounced   FLUM - ARY   (with u as in plum, a as in ago and y as in duty)

Origin
Flummery is from the Welsh **llymru** meaning *harsh* or *raw.* Originally, it was an acid-sharp jelly made from the husks of oats, left-over bits of little importance. It came to mean anything of little significance - a trifle.

Meaning
Flummery is a fluffy, cold dessert made with milk, eggs, sugar and flour (or an oatmeal jelly), which is often flavoured with fruit.

Associations
see: dessert

Foie gras

Pronounced   FWA -GRA (with a's as in cat)

Origin
Foie is French for **liver** and **gras** for *fat.* **Foie gras** is   literally *fat liver.*   Dishes made from the livers of fattened geese were eaten in Ancient Rome and Ancient Greece. Périgueux, Strasbourg and Toulouse are well-known for the superb quality of their foie gras.

Meaning
Foie gras is obtained from geese and ducks which have been force fed (called **le garage** in France, meaning *cramming*) on a special diet in a confined living space, until they are grossly fat and their livers have become enlarged and fatty.

The livers of some fattened geese and ducks weigh as much as 2 kilograms. The best foie gras, which is creamy-white tinged with pink, is firm and comes from Alsace and from the Dordogne area of South West France. The best **foie gras** is **foie gras entier** which consists of only liver; **foie gras morceau**, which has small bits of foie gras with other meat, is of a lesser quality. **Foie gras** should not be confused with **pâté de foie**, which is usually made from pork or other meat. Pâté de foie is much less expensive than foie gras. Foie gras is usually served as an appetizer, an hors d'oeuvre, an entrée or as an accompaniment to some meat dishes.

Associations
see: **appetizer, charcuterie, entrée, hors d'oeuvre, pâté**

foie gras

Fondue

Pronounced   FON-DU (with o as in on and u as in future)

Origin
Fondue is from the Latin **fundere** meaning *to pour* and from the French **fondre** meaning *to melt.* **Fondant** is French for *melting* and also a bonbon which melts in the mouth.   tomato fondue

Meaning

Fondue has a number of meanings. One is the resultant mixture after vegetables have been cooked in butter until they are reduced to a pulp. Another is a dish consisting of scrambled eggs and melted cheese. **Swiss fondue**, of which there is a great variety (cheese, beef, tomato, fish and desserts, such as chocolate) is traditionally made with melted cheese cooked in a **caquelon**, an earthenware pot which allows the cheese to cook slowly, as overheating makes the cheese become stringy. It is cooked with a dry white wine (e.g. graves) and sometimes a white cherry brandy called kirsch. Each diner takes a long fondue fork with long prongs to spear pieces of bread which are dipped in the pot. Another fondue is that where each diner at table has a fondue dish of hot butter and oil with its own stand and heater. Each diner spears cubes of meat which are cooked to their liking in the oil and then dipped into one of a variety of sauces. **Fondue** should not be confused with **fondant**, which is a soft confection, something like fudge, which is often used as an icing or a sweet.

Associations

Fonduta is Italian for *melted cheese* - in the dish *cheese on toast.*
see: raclette, ramekin, sukiyaki

Fool

Pronounced   FOOL (with oo as in moon)

Origin

Fool is from the Latin **follis** and later the Middle English **fol** meaning a *bellows* and later a *wind-bag* or *empty-headed person.* The dish was probably called fool because it was light and airy and a mere trifle.

Meaning

A **fool** consists of almost any kind of fruit, which is cooked in a small amount of water and made into a purée. Sugar is added to it and it is refrigerated. Whipped cream (or custard) is added in the proportion of 2 of cream to 1 of purée, which produces a creamy liquid. It can be served in a sherbet glass or coupe. **Gooseberry** and **rhubarb fools** are well-known English desserts.

Associations
see: dessert, purée

Frankfurter

Pronounced   FRANK - FURTA
(with first a as in pan, u as in fur and
final a as in ago)

Origin

From the Middle Ages (10th century on-
wards), it has been customary to name
dishes with the name of the place in
which they originate. As one would expect, the **frankfurter**
sausage originated in Frankfurt-on-Main in Germany

Meaning

A **frankfurter** is a sausage about 10 cms long which is made
from ground pork. It is lightly smoked and has a distinctive, mild
taste. In Germany, it is served with sauerkraut (choucroute). In
the U.S.A., and increasingly throughout the world, it is used to

make a **hotdog,** which is a hot frankfurter inside a long soft bread-roll. Often the hotdog includes fried onions and a sauce. It is usually eaten as a snack.

Associations
see: **sausage, wurst**

Fricassée

Pronounced   FRIK-A-SAY (with i as in pick, a as in ago and ay as in day)

Origin
Fricassée is from the French   **fricasser** meaning *to cut up.* It came to mean meat *cut up into small pieces.*

Meaning
The word **fricassée** usually refers to a white stew or ragoût which consists of chicken (or small birds), rabbit , lamb or veal which has been cut up into small pieces and braised. It is also used in the sense of previously-cooked meat which is warmed up with a white sauce.

Associations
see: **ragoût, rechauffé, vol au vent**

Galantine

Pronounced GALAN-TEEN (with a's as in cat and ee as in see)

Origin
Galantine derives from either the Old French géline or galine which meant a chicken, because the dish was first made with poultry, or from the Latin gelatina meaning jelly. In the 17th century, the dish was made with meat, fish and a variety of birds.

Meaning

A **galantine** is usually white meat from veal or a bird (e.g. poultry) which has been boned, stuffed with forcemeat, cooked in a **gelatine** (jelly) stock in a cooking cloth and then pressed into a required shape. Sometimes, it is glazed and finished with a topping of toasted breadcrumbs. It is left after cooking to go cold and for the jelly to set and it is then usually cut into slices.

Associations

see: **aspic, ballotine, charcuterie,chaud-froid**

Game

Pronounced   GAM (with a as in came)

Origin

Game is from the Old English word **gamen** meaning *sport.* A common sport or pastime for the rich in days past was to hunt wild animals. The word game changed with time from the activity to the prey that was caught.

Meaning

Game today usually refers to fairly small wild animals which by law can be hunted only at certain seasons (excluding rabbits and pigeons) . They are small enough to be readily dealt with in a kitchen and include duck, guinea fowl, partridge, pheasant, quail, spatchcock and woodcock.

Associations

In France, a **crapaudine** is a *spatchcock* (a small chicken) which is split down the middle of its back, flattened out and then grilled. One of the most famous of game dishes is **duck à l'orange** which is roast duck served with an orange-flavoured sauce.

Gammon

Pronounced GAM-AN (with the first a as in cat and the second as in ago)

Origin

Gammon derives from the Old Norman French word **gambe** meaning *leg*. It referred to the bottom piece of a flitch of ham, including the hind leg. The word **ham** was Old English for a *hog's thigh salted and dried*. The Gauls, the inhabitants of what is now France, are said to have first cured pork to produce ham.

Meaning

Gammon is **ham**. It is a leg or shoulder of pork which is either cured by salting or smoking, or left *"green "* or raw.

Associations

The French for **gammon** or **ham** is **jambon,** of which there are a number of varieties (**jambon cru** - *raw,* **fumé** - *smoked* and **blanc**- *boiled* and *mildly cured*). **Bayonne** in the South West of France is famous for its hams, which are usually eaten raw. The most famous English ham is **York ham**, which is boiled

and usually slightly salted. The best-known Italian ham (called **prosciutto** in Italian) is that from Parma. It is a smoked, uncooked ham which is sliced paper-thin and eaten with figs or melon. The most famous German ham is **Westphalian ham** which, like prosciutto, is usually eaten raw in very thin slices. In the U.S.A., it is generally recognised that the finest hams are from **Kentucky** and **Smithfield.**
see: **charcuterie, hollandaise, prosciutto, piperade**

Garam masala

Pronounced GARAM (with first a as in ago, the next as in father MASALA (with the first and last a's in masala as in ago and the middle a as in far)

Origin
Garam is Hindi (Indian) for *warm* or *hot* and **masala** for a spice *mixture.* **Garam masala** literally means *hot spices.*

Meaning
Garam masala is a blend of ground spices and herbs which is used as a basis for all Indian curries. The condiment is the prototype of **curry powder** available in shops but in India the various spices are added individually to a dish at precisely the right moment. A garam masala can be dry or wet. When it is wet, a liquid, such as coconut milk or water, is added. A garam masala usually consists of a bay leaf, black cummin, black pepper, cardamon, cinnamon, cloves, coriander and nutmeg. This produces a very fragrant and aromatic blend. The garam masala itself is not hot as it contains no chillis but a dish can be made mild or hot according to one's taste by the addition of chillis and peppers. The garam masala should be added to a dish in the final minutes of cooking a curry.

Associations
A **masala** is also a blend of spices but the blend is made by choosing some spices from the hundreds available. Indian cooks vary their masalas according to the dish they are making and they are usually a matter of individual preference and so vary widely.
see: **curry, tandoori**

Garnish

Pronounced GAR-NISH (with a as in garden and i as in fish)

Origin
Garnish is derived from an Old French word **garnir** meaning *to fortify* or *provide protection.* It came to mean anything that was provided not to protect but to embellish or adorn and then to food which was added to a dish to decorate it and make it more attractive, colourful and palatable. Garnishes have often been named afer a place, an important occasion or, most often, after a person who originated or inspired them.

Meaning
The term **garnish** is usually used in cuisine for savoury dishes. Desserts and sweet dishes are **decorated**. A garnish is an edible embellishment to a dish to improve its appearance. There are literally hundreds of garnishes for different dishes. What one uses as a garnish depends upon one's taste and culinary creativity, although there are traditional garnishes for some classic dishes (see **coq au vin** and **beef bourguinnone**). A basic pizza, for instance, can be garnished by chopped beef or ham, mushrooms, salami, peppers, prawns, anchovies, etc. A veal dish might be garnished with olives, capers and lemons. An omelette might simply be garnished with the feathery fronds of dill or fennel. There are no rules and regulations related to garnishes and cooks throughout the ages have always experimented with new ways of presenting food.

Associations
Garni is the French for *garnished,* as in **choucroute garni** (*sauerkraut with sausages*). If the word **dianne** (the goddess of the moon and of hunting) is used to describe a dish, it indicates that the dish will be garnished with *crescent-shaped croûtons.* In South East Asia, cooks often reveal artistry and grace in shaping vegetables and fruits to produce the most delightfully-shaped garnishes.
see: á la (jardinière, e.g.), bouquet garni, fleuron, marron, mirepoix, miso, nasi goreng, navarin, quenelle, raclette, rice, sauerkraut, seaweed, teriyaki, tournedos

Gastronome

Pronounced GA-STRA-NOM (with first a as in cat, second as in ago and o as in over)

Origin
The Ancient Greek for *stomach* was **gaster** and **nomos** meant *to arrange*. From these words developed **gastronomy**, literally *the arranging of food for the stomach*, which became *the art and science of good eating* (that is putting good things into the stomach). The word **gastronome** was first used in France at the beginning of the 19th century.

Meaning
A **gastronome** has a number of meanings. In France, it means someone who writes about or judges good food. In France and other countries, it also means someone who enjoys, appreciates and is knowledgable about fine food.

Associations
A **gastronom** in Russia is a luxury food shop. A **gourmet** is a connoisseur of good food and fine wine. A **gourmand**, however, (which is sometimes confused with a gourmet) is a glutton; someone who eats excessively. The Italian for gourmet is **buongustai** and the German **feinschmeker**, which literally mean *fine taste*.
see: epicure, truffle

Gâteau

Pronounced GA-TO (with a as in cat and o as in over)

Origin
Gâteau is French for *cake*. It derives from the Old French word **gastel** which meant *a delicate food which quickly deteriorates*. The modern French word **gater**, meaning *to spoil,* is related.

Meaning
The word **gâteau** (plural **gâteaux**) refers to all kinds of small and large cakes and to pastries, whereas **dessert** refers to dishes

such as tarts, flans, fritters, cream delicacies, charlottes and different kinds of ices. Many countries have special gâteaux which are eaten on feast days, festivals and special occasions (such as weddings) in families. For example, in France they have a **Twelfth Night cake** (*gâteau des Rois*). In many English-speaking countries, they have **Christmas cake.** Russia has its **Easter cake** (*kulich*), as does Germany (*östertorte*). One of the best- known and liked gâteaux in the world is the **German Black Forest cherry cake** (*Schwarzwalder kirschtorte*).

Associations
The Italian for gâteau or cake is **torta** and **tortina.** In Spanish it is **torta.**
see: choux, panettone, savarin, stollen, torte

Gazpacho

Pronounced GAS-PACHO (with a's as in cat and o as in go)

Origin
Gazpacho derives from an Arabic word meaning *soaked bread.*

The dish is mentioned in Ancient Greek and Roman literature and in the Old and New Testaments of the Bible.

Meaning

Gazpacho is a cold, refreshing summer soup. It is made from skinned and seeded tomatoes and peppers, which are pounded in a mortar, garlic, olive oil, vinegar, seasoning and iced water. After this mixture has marinated for 30 minutes, paper-thin slices of cucumber and slices of thin bread (less often nowadays) and cubes of ice are added. It is refrigerated and then served very cold.

Associations

Khlodnik is an iced soup which is very popular in Poland and Russia. **Cocido** from Central Spain is a similar soup.

Gelato

Pronounced
JAY-LA-TO (with ay as in say, a as in father and o as in over)

Origin

The Chinese knew the art of making flavoured water ices (sherbets) almost two thousand years ago. The Indians, Arabs and Persians learned the art from them and traders from these countries passed on the process to Europeans. Ice cream became popular among the rich in the 17th century in Europe. **Gelato** is derived from the Latin **gelare** meaning *to freeze* or *stiffen*. It is now Italian for ice cream.

Meaning
Gelato (plural **gelati**) is ice cream made from egg yolks, granulated sugar, milk or cream and a little salt which is blended with a purée of fruit, a liqueur or an essence to give flavour. It is then refrigerated at the maximum freezing point. When it is ready for serving, it should be stiff but still creamy. Popular gelati are **gelato di vaniglia** (vanilla), **gelato di fragole** (strawberry), **gelato di caffé** (coffee), **gelato di nocciole** (hazelnut) and **gelato di albicocche** (apricot). In Italy gelati are sold in a **gelataria** (an ice cream parlour).

Associations
The French for ice cream is **glace** (e.g. **glace au citron** and **glace à l'orange**).
See: **cassata, granite, sorbet**

Ghee

Pronounced
GEE (with ee as in see). In India, it is pronounced KEE (with ee as in see).

Origin
Ghee is from the Hindi (Indian) word **ghi** meaning *clarified butter.*

Meaning
Ghee is pure, clarified butter fat which is prepared from the milk of buffalo. When the butter fat is gently heated in a pan, sediments sink to the bottom of the pan and the clarified ghee can be poured off. The ghee has its own distinctive fragrance and flavour. It is very useful for cooking, as it will not burn at high temperatures. It is as popular in Indian, Middle East and Asian cuisine as olive oil is in Greek, Spanish and Italian cuisine.

Associations
Ghee is called **samna** in Arabic.
see: **naan, parantha**

Gnocchi

Pronounced N'YOK-EE (with o as in go and ee as in see)

Origin

Gnocchi is Italian for *dumplings.* In one shape or another, dumplings have been eaten for thousands of years in most countries. The Ancient Romans ate them as part of their daily fare.

Meaning

Gnocchi alla Roma are dumplings made usually from semolina bound into a paste with egg and then baked in an oven in milk, seasoning and a pinch of nutmeg. **Gnocchi di patate** are dumplings made from cooked potatoes and flour. **Gnocchi di ricotta** are dumplings made with ricotta cheese and flour. Ricotta cheese is a soft, white, fairly salty curd made from whey and skimmed milk. **Gnocchi verdi** (**verdi** being Italian for *green*) is a speciality of Northern Italy and is made from spinach, flour and ricotta cheese. Gnocchi are traditionally served with **polenta** in Northern Italy but they are also served with stew or with meat and fish dishes.

Associations

French gnocchi, called **noques,** are made from choux pastry with a cheese flavouring.
see: **choux, dumpling, polenta, semolina**

Goulash

goulash

Pronounced GOO-LASH (with oo as in moon and a as in cash)

Origin

Goulash is from the Hungarian **gulyas** meaning *of a herdsman* from **gulya** meaning *to herd.* It describes a style of cooking similar to the hunter style (**cacciatore** and **chausseur**) in Italian and French cuisine.

Meaning
Goulash is prepared by stewing beef (or, less often, pork), spiced with **paprika** (hungarian red pepper), with onions, tomatoes and sometimes sliced potatoes and mushrooms. It is traditionally topped with sour cream and sprinkled with a little more paprika. It is often served with boiled potatoes .

Associations
Szeged goulash is goulash served with sauerkraut.
see: **casserole, cacciatore (and chasseur), sauerkraut**

Granite

Pronounced
GRAN-EETAY (with a as in father, ee as in see and ay as in say)

Origin
Granite is the Italian for a *water ice.* In Italian **granito** means *granite* (a very hard stone) or *grained*, as does the word **granité** in French.

Meaning
Granite (singular **granita**) are light water ices (**sorbets**) made in Italy from finely-powdered ice and a sugar syrup which is flavoured with lemon, strawberry, coffee and other flavours. The flavoured syrups are frozen in a deep freeze and are never stirred. This results in the granite having a grainy texture .

Associations
In France, these water ices are called **granités**.
see: **bombe, cassata, parfait, sorbet**

Gratinée

Pronounced
GRAT-INAY (with a as in fat, i as in pin and ay as in say)

Origin
In French, **gratin** means *the burnt portion sticking to the side*

of a pan. A dish which is **gratinée**, or in English **gratin**, means it is glazed and has a browned, crusty surface.

Meaning
Gratinée or **gratin** describes a dish, the top of which has been covered with bread crumbs and/or grated cheese and has then been subjected to high heat either under a grill or from a blow - torch to produce a crisp, golden-brown crust on the dish. This process is called **au gratin**, as in **macaroni au gratin, potato cheese au gratin, scallops au gratin** and **cauliflower au gratin.**

Associations
The Italian for **gratinée** is **gratinato.**
see: **lasagne, macaroni, mousse, noodles, sauce mornay**

Grissini

Pronounced GREES -SEE-NEE
(with ee's as in see)

Origin
Grissini is Italian for *bread sticks.* They are a speciality of Turin.

Meaning
Grissini are long, thin sticks of crisp bread which have been baked hard. They vary in length from about 25 to 27 centimetres. They are served as a snack or to accompany soups or dips.

Associations
see: **bagna cauda**

Guacamole

Pronounced GWAKA-MO-LAY (with first a as in cat, second a as in ago, o as in over and ay as in say)

Origin
Guacamole is Spanish for **avocado sauce**. The **avocado** (or **avocado pear**) was first harvested in Mexico by the Aztecs before 300 B.C. It originated in Central and South America and was taken to Spain by the conquerors of the Aztecs in the early 1600's.

Meaning
Guacamole (or **guacamol**) is made from mashed avocado mixed with chopped tomatoes and onions, olive oil, seasoning, chilli and a dash of tabasco. It is often sprinkled with fresh coriander. It is served in Mexico and Spain with tortilla dishes, frijoles and some meat dishes. It can be used as a dip, a sauce, a garnish or simply by itself.

Associations
see: garnish, tortilla

Gumbo

Pronounced   GUM-BO (with u as in rum and o as in over)

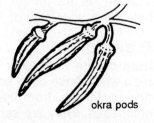
okra pods

Origin
Gumbo is from the African **ngumbo** meaning *okra,* which is known to have been used in cooking in Ancient Egypt over 2000 years ago. It originated in North East Africa and was carried in slave ships to the West Indies and then to America and to the Middle East countries by traders and then later to Europe and North and South America.

Meaning
Okra or **gumbo** (or **quingumbo**) is a vegetable whose pods resemble a haricot bean. They are shaped like long fingers and

are also called **lady's fingers** and **bunya beans**. Okra grows now in South America, the Southern parts of the United States, West and North Africa and India, where it is an ingredient in many dishes. The pods are eaten when young and fresh and should be steeped in water before they are boiled, steamed or fried as a separate vegetable or as part of a savoury dish. Gumbo refers also to a dish served with **okra**. It is particularly popular in some of the southern states of the U.S.A. (particularly the Cajun-Creole cuisine of Louisiana), where gumbo has become a casserole-type of dish, which includes a great variety of fish and seafoods as well as vegetables and Cajun-Creole spicy sauces. Okra is particularly good for stews and casseroles as it exudes a thick juice which thickens and enriches them.

Associations
see: Cajun-Creole,   casserole

Hamburger

Pronounced   HAM-BURGA (with first a as in cat, u as in fur and final a as in ago)

Origin

It is probable that the term **hamburger** originated in the mid 1800's when German immigrants to the United States sailed on the Hamburg-Amerika liners. As salted, smoked beef from Hamburg kept well on the voyage, much of it was used as food. As the meat was hard when dry, it was minced and some onions and (to eke it out) some soaked breadcrumbs were added. The dish was palatable and became popular with the immigrant, who continued to eat it when they settled in the United States.

Meaning

A **hamburger** consists of a ground beef pattie, fried onions and sauce (e.g. worcester or tomato) served inside a yeast bun, which is sprinkled on top with seeds (caraway, poppy, celery or sesame). They are also sold in fast-food restaurants containing a salad of lettuce, sliced tomatoes and raw or cooked onion rings. Hamburgers are eaten as snacks or as a main meal in a busy day.

Hollandaise

Pronounced HOLAN-DAYZ (with o as in hot, a as in ago and ay as in say)

Origin

Hollandaise is French for *Dutch.* The sauce, which originated in Holland, has been a favourite sauce in the repertoire of many chefs for over two hundred years.

Meaning

Hollandaise is a rich sauce made from reduced wine vinegar, seasoning, egg yolks, butter and, at the last moment, lemon juice. It is usually made in a bain marie, to avoid any curdling. It is served hot with eggs, fish and vegetables. It is very popular in Europe with fresh asparagus (green or white), which has been very lightly poached or steamed. Another popular dish is **eggs benedict**, consisting of toasted muffins on which are slices of ham which are topped with poached eggs and then covered with hollandaise sauce.

Associations

One meaning of **chantilly** is a hollandaise sauce to which whipped cream has been added.

see: bain marie, béarnaise, gammon, mousseline

Hors d' oeuvre

Pronounced HOR - DURV (with o as in horse and u as in fur)

hors d'oeuvres platter

Origin

Hors is French for outside   and **oeuvre** for work or working. In cuisine, it was coined to mean *something eaten outside* and *before the normal meal.* **Hors d'oeuvres** were developed by French chefs in Russia in the 17th century, when the Russian aristocracy was very much influenced by things French. At that time the Russian aristocracy had elaborate dinners with many guests, so many in fact that the receptions to welcome them took a very long time.   During this waiting period before the meal

119

began numerous guests consumed large quantities of wine and spirits, often with intoxicating effects on empty stomachs. Consequently, a form of eating before the main meal began was introduced - the hors d'oeuvre - which helped to keep many of the guests a little more sober.

Meaning
Hors d'oeuvres are light, delicate, hot or cold and varied savoury snacks or appetizers. They are served before a meal begins to whet and excite the appetite rather than satisfy it, so they should not be too rich or heavy and the portions should be very small. Usually they are accompanied by an **aperatif,** an alcholic appetizer. Sometimes the hors d'oeuvres are laid out on table and the guests help themselves or they are handed out on raviers (which are small oblong hors d'oeuvres dishes), or from trays or trolleys.

Associations
In Italy an **hors d'oeuvre** is called **antipasto**, in Germany **vorspeise**, in Japan **zensai**, in Russia **zakuska**, in Turkey and Balkan countries **mezes. Salpicon** consists of small, diced ingredients which are bound with a sauce and used as a filling in various pastry cases as hors d'oeuvres. In Germany they have a **schwedenplatte** which consists of different hors d'oeuvres with a foundation of fish.

see: **antipasto, appetizer, barquette, blini, brioche, brochette, canapés, cassolette, caviar, charcuterie, choux, croissant, croustades, croûtes, croquettes, croûton, dim sum, felafel, foie gras, fritters, mortadella, pâté, patties, prosciutto , quiche, rillette, rissoles, rollmops, salami, tahini, taramasalata, terrine vol au vent, wurst**

Julienne

Pronounced JOO-LEE-EN (with oo as in soon, ee as in see and en as in pen)

Origin
The manner of cutting vegetables in the form of **Julienne** is attributed to Jean Julien, a French chef of the 18th century.

Meaning

The term **julienne** means that vegetables, such as carrots, are cut lengthwise into thin and narrow strips. They often form an attractive garnish to dishes. The term can apply also (less often) to meat (such as cooked ham) which is finely sliced. In French cuisine, a **julienne** also means a consommé to which is added tender, finely-shredded vegetables, such as carrots, turnips, celery, onions and the heart of lettuce.

Associations

see: **consommé, garnish**

Kebab

Pronounced KI-BAB (with i as in pin and a as in rabbit)

Origin

Kebab or **kabob** is Turkish for *cooked beef*. The kebab, or shish-kebab, originated in Turkey over two thousand years ago. In Turkish **sis** means a *sword* from which **shish** derives meaning *on a skewer.* Mutton, lamb or buffalo, cut into squares, were seasoned, grilled on a skewer (sometimes on a sword) over an open fire or grill.

Meaning

Nowadays **kebab** (also spelled **kabob** and **khubab**) means any meat, seafood or poultry which is cut into about bite-size portions, seasoned and then cooked on a skewer. Often vegetables, such as tomatoes, mushrooms and peppers are placed between pieces of meat on a skewer and then the kebab is grilled. It is served by itself or with a garnish.

Associations

In Turkey and Greece, and increasingly in many countries throughout the world, shops have **döner kebabs**, which are vertical grills holding seasoned lamb which rotates before a charcoal fire. Originally, a whole leg of lamb was used for the doner kebab; nowadays, it often consists of minced lamb mixed with herbs which is formed into a leg shape. Slices of lamb are taken from the well-cooked outside of the large piece of lamb on the grill and served in some form of bread.

In France, skewered meat, like a kebab, is called a **brochette**, in Russia a **shashlik** and in the Middle East a **kabob**. Chicken kebabs, called **yakitori**, are very popular in Japan, as are **cavap**, which are lamb kebabs, in Jugoslavia.

see: naan, parantha, satay

Kedgeree

Pronounced   KED-JAREE (with e as in fed, a as in ago and ee as in see)

Origin

Kedgeree derives from the Hindi word **khichi** meaning *a dish of rice, split peas, onions and eggs.* It was a popular breakfast dish among well-to-do English people both in India and England in the 19th century and later.

Meaning

Kedgeree is a fish and rice dish consisting of boiled or grilled smoked or fresh haddock, long-grained rice, seasoning, curry powder and a dash of paprika. The mixture is garnished with chopped, hard-boiled eggs and chopped parsley. Sometimes curried minced meat and curried shredded vegetables and dhal

(split peas) are added. The dish is popular in India and makes a filling and tasty main course served with fresh vegetables or a salad.

Associations
see: **curry, dhal, rice, salad**

Korma

Pronounced KOOR-MA (with oo as in soon and a as in far)

Origin
Korma or **quoorma** is a Tamil word meaning *to braise.*

Meaning
Traditionally, a **korma** is a casserole of curried lamb or mutton made with a thick sauce. It consists of one centimetre squares of lamb or mutton, shallots, onions, garlic, a little sugar and

seasoning, rice flour and spices (such as coriander, peppers, cardamon, cloves, etc.). Stock is added and tumeric and almond milk. It can be thickened when almost ready with pounded nuts or yoghurt. A little lemon is added just before serving. Nowadays, there are also prawn and chicken kormas. They are usually served with naan and rice.

Associations
see: **casserole, naan, stock, yoghurt**

Kugelhopf

Pronounced KOOGAL-HOF
with oo as in moon, a as in ago and o
as in go

Origin
A **kuge** is German for a *ball* and **hopf** means *hops*, a plant which gives the bitter flavour to malt used in the making of beer. The **kugelhopf** originated in Austria. It is said to have been a favourite dessert of Queen Marie Antoinette of France (1756 - 1793).

Meaning
A **kugelhopf** (also called a **kouglof** and a **gougelhopf)** is a yeast cake which is usually made in a round, flat-topped mould with fluted sides. A mould is lined with shredded almonds and then it is filled with dough made with sieved flour, yeast, fine sugar, butter, eggs, currants and a little salt. It is baked in an oven for about 45 minutes.

Associations
In Russia, a kugelhopf is called **kulich** and in Poland it is called **babka.** The Italian version is **panettone**
see: **baba, brioche, gâteau, savarin**

Lamington

Pronounced LAMIN-TAN
(with first a as in man, i as in tin and final a as in ago)

Australia

Darwin

Queensland

Brisbane

Perth

Adelaide

Sydney

Canberra

Melbourne

Hobart

Origin
The lamington is said to have been named after Lord Lamington, the governor of the state of Queensland in Australia from 1895 to 1901.

Meaning
The **lamington** is one of Australia's best-known cakes. It consists of 4 cm squares of sponge cake. Each square is dipped into warm chocolate on all sides and then drained. The squares are then rolled in coconut and left to cool and set.

Lasagne

Pronounced   LA-SAN -YA (with the first two a's as in cat and the final a as in ago)

Origin
Lasagne is Italian for *broad-leafed.*   The Italians used this word to describe a wide ribbon-shaped pasta. Over two thousand years ago, the Chinese made long wide ribbons of pasta, which they laid out in the sun to dry. Marco Polo, a Venetian traveller who was befriended by the Great Khan, the emperor of China, probably brought back the process of making lasagne to Italy from China in 1295 .

Meaning
Lasagne is made from lasagne pasta, which is plain or green (*verde* in Italian) and a sauce of minced beef, tomato purée, seasoning and garlic. The lasagne is boiled in water with a touch of oil until it is **al dente**. It is then drained. In a shallow, oven-proof dish, the pasta and the sauce are layered, finishing with a layer of meat. This is then baked. Cheese or a cheese sauce is then placed over the meat and the dish is returned to the oven until the dish has gratinéed.

Associations
see: gratinée, pasta, al and alla (*al dente*)

Macaroni

Pronounced MAKA-RO-NY (with first a as in cat, second a as in ago, o as in over and y as in duty)

Origin
Macaroni comes from the Old Italian word **maccaroni**, meaning **to crush**, which derives from the Greek **makaria** meaning *barley food.* Originally, the word meant pounded wheat or barley and then later a wheat paste formed into tubes. Originally, **macaroni** was the generic term for all **pasta**. It was probably first made in Sicily.

Meaning
Macaroni is a farinaceous (starchy) food of the large pasta family. It consists of small tubular pieces of pasta about 1 cm wide. It is cooked, like other pasta, in salted boiling water (with a drop or two of oil) for about 10 to 20 minutes and, like all pasta, should not be overcooked but should be **al dente**. It can be served plainly with a little melted butter or be part of a combined dish, such as **macaroni cheese** (*macaroni au gratin*).

see: al dente (in al and alla), gratinée, pasta, spaghetti

Macédoine

Pronounced   MASAY-DWAN (with a's as in cat and ay as in say)

Origin
Macédoine derives from the ancient kingdom of **Macedonia** (now partly Greece and Turkey), a country which was formed by a number of small states. The dish macédoine is formed from a number of small (chopped up) fruits or vegetables.

Meaning
A **macédoine** is a mixture of raw or cooked fruit or vegetables, which are diced into evenly-sized bits and often used as a garnish. A **macédoine of fruit** is a fruit salad comprising slices of fruit such as bananas, pears, apricots and berries, such as raspberries and strawberries. The fruit is immersed in a sugar syrup. Sometimes it is also flavoured with a liqueur and set in a jelly. It is served as a dessert.

Associations
Similar to the **macédoine of fruit** is the German **obst salat** (*fruit salad*).
see: **compoté,   dessert, garnish, salad**

Madeleine

Pronounced   MAD-LAYN (with a as in far and ay as in say)

Origin
Various views have been expressed regarding which person first *made* **madeleines**. They were popular in the early 18th century in France. The name **Madeleine** (the French for *Magdalen)* was given to the cake by Antonin Carême (1784-1833), one of the most famous of French chefs.

Meaning

Madeleines are small, sponge cakes, made from a *genoise* mixture, which are baked in a scallop-shaped mould or in **dariole** (a small mould) tins. They are coated with apricot or raspberry jam and are then rolled in desiccated coconut. The little cakes are decorated with glacé cherries or diamonds of angelica.

Maître d' hôtel

Pronounced
MAYTRA -DOTEL (with ay as in say and a as in ago, o as in over and e as in egg)

Origin
Maître is French for *master*. **Maître d'hôtel** literally means *master of the hotel*. It came to mean the **head waiter** in a restaurant.

Meaning
A **maître d'hôtel** is the person in charge of a dining room in a hotel or restaurant. He is also competent to prepare some dishes at a table. He usually has under his charge a number of waiters and waitresses.

Associations
In French, **commis** means *assistant*. In a large restaurant, the person in charge of the wine cellar and the serving of wine in the restaurant is called the **sommelier**.
see: **beurre (maître d'hôtel), pomme, restaurant**

Marengo

Pronounced
MAREN-GO (with a as in far, e as in pen and o as in over)

Origin
The dish **marengo** is said to have been produced by Monsieur Dunant, the Swiss chef of Napoleon (1769 - 182), following Bonaparte's victory over the Austrians at the **Battle of Morengo** in Northern Italy on 14 June, 1800. The chef is said

to have obtained all the ingredients for the dish from produce gathered in the surrounding countryside.

Meaning
Marengo usually describes a chicken dish. It consists of sautéed chicken, which, traditionally, is topped with a garnish of crayfish pieces and fried eggs. It is accompanied by a sauce made from garlic, oil, tomatoes, mushrooms, water and a little brandy. The dish is also made with sautéed veal.

Associations
see: **poularde**

Marinade

Pronounced
MARIN-AD (with the first a as in mat, i as in pin and the second a as in made)

Origin
Marinade is from the Spanish **marinar** meaning *pickle in brine.* Originally, the word meant only a pickle of wine or vinegar with spices added.

Meaning
A **marinade** nowadays is more than a pickle solution. It is a strongly-flavoured liquid in which gashed (to allow the liquid to penetrate easily) meat and fish are **marinated** (*steeped*) until they get the flavour of the marinade. The process also tends to tenderise some tough cuts of meat or game. For example, beef may be marinated in a marinade of red wine, olive oil, parsley, grated nutmeg, all spice, bay leaf and salt for about 12 hours before being cooked. Gammon may be marinated in a dry white wine, olive oil, lemon juice and a bay leaf for about 12 hours before being cooked. Mushrooms marinated in a marinade of water, olive oil, lemon juice, garlic, bay leaf, peppercorns and salt are frequently part of antipasto dishes. A bay leaf is excellent for all marinades. In France, if a marinade has been boiled and then cooled, it is called a **marinade cuite** (*cook*ed) if not it is called a **marinade crue** (*raw*).

Associations
The process of steeping food in an aromatic liquid is also called

maceration. In Fijii, **kokoda** is a dish of raw fish which has been marinated in lime juice. **Seviche** is a South American dish where raw fish is *"cooked "* in lemon and lime juices, as is **poisson crud** in Tahiti. **Gravalax** is a Swedish speciality of raw salmon cured with sugar, all-spice and seasoning and served with a mustard sauce.

see: antipasto, daube, gammon, rollmop, sashimi, sauerbrauten, teriyaki, vindaloo

---

Marinara

Pronounced   MAREE-NARA (with a's as in far and ee as in see)

pasta marinara

Origin
A **marinaro** is Italian for a *sailor* and **marinara**   for *in the manner of a sailor.* The use of the term marinara is a fanciful way of saying that a dish uses food from the sea.

Meaning
A dish cooked **marinara** has a sauce which includes tomatoes, garlic, olive oil and oregano - and fish or seafood . The dish is popular in Italian cuisine, e.g. **spaghetti marinara**.

Marmite petite

Pronounced MAR-MEET PE-TEET (with a as in cat, ee's as in see and e as in pet)

Origin
Marmite is French for a **metal o r earthenware stockpot** with or without feet and with handles on each side. Nowadays, it also means a double-cooking pan. **Petite** is French for *small.*

Meaning
A **marmite petite** is the name of a clear, savoury soup, which is cooked and served in a **marmite**.

Associations
see: **consommé, pot au feu**

Marron

Pronounced MA-RON (with a as in cat and on as in song)

Origin
Marron is French for a large, edible and specially-cultivated *s w e e t chestnut.* The **sweet chestnut tree,** which is entirely different from a **chestnut tree** (which does not have edible nuts), originated in Europe and was introduced into Britain by the Ancient Romans.

Meaning
The supply of **marrons** throughout the world comes from France and Italy, where they are commercially grown.   Marrons are usually avail-

chocolate chestnut cream

able from gourmet stores in tins   in either a natural or pickled form. They are used in paste form as an ingredient in dessert dishes, as garnishes, cooked with meats, in stuffings and purées and are used in cakes and meringues. Chestnuts roasted on a grill (often in the open air) are very popular in some countries, especially those which have very cold winters. **Marrons glacées** are marrons glazed (candied)   with sugar, which are eaten as confections or used in desserts.

Associations

Monte Bianco (in French **Mont Blanc** -the highest peak in the French Alps) is an Italian dessert consisting of puréed marrons which are piped through a cone so that a delicate mountain is formed, which is then given a white summit of rum-flavoured whipped cream. A dish of Chestnuts with boiled brussel sprouts was the favourite meal of Goethe, the famous German poet.

In Western Australia, a **marron** is a **yabbie**, which is a fresh-water crayfish.

see: dessert, garnish, polenta, purée

Marzipan

Pronounced   MA-ZI-PAN (with first a as in father, i as in pin and final a as in can)

Origin

Marzipan was originally called **marche pane**. Its origins are obscure. The word **marzipan** is from the Ger-man. The marzipan mixture originated in the Middle East where almonds and cane sugar grew in profusion. It was popular in Persia (now Iran) in A.D. 965. It was brought to Europe by Arabs and by Crusaders and became very popular for many sweet dishes. Lübeck in the far north of Germany became a centre for the manufacture of marzipan in the 16th century and has remained so to this day. Marzipan sweets and desserts are a particular favourite of the Germans.

Meaning

Marzipan is made from almonds which have been pounded into a paste to which are added egg whites and sugar flavoured with rose or orange-flower water. It is used to make confections and as an ingredient in cakes, biscuits and desserts. It is manufactured on a large scale in Belgium, Germany and Holland, countries which, at festival times, mould marzipan into the forms of animals, fruit, vegetables and other intricate shapes.

Associations

In French, marzipan is **massepain** and in Italian it is **marzpane**.
see: almond, dessert

Mayonnaise

Pronounced
MAY-ONAYZ (with ay's as in say and o as in gone)

Origin
There are four versions of the origin of **mayonnaise**. The first is that it took its name from the place from which it originated, which was **Mahon** in the small Spanish island of Minorca. The second is that it was invented in the town of Bayonne in the area of Basses-Pyrénées in the South West of France. The third is that it derives from an Old French word **moyeu** meaning *egg yolks.* The fourth is that the Duke of Alla Mayenne at the Battle of Arques, on learning that for lunch he was to have only an ungarnished cold chicken, called his chef to him and spent so much time to originate a sauce for the dish that the battle was lost - but a new sauce was born.

Meaning
Mayonnaise is a dressing consisting mainly of cooking oil (e.g. olive oil), egg yolks (to stablilise the emulsion), lemon juice or vinegar and seasoning. It is not cooked but is mixed at room temperature. The ingredients, other than the oil, should be whisked vigorously and then the oil should be added drop by drop very slowly, with continuous beating of the mixture. It should be as smooth as cream and be glossy. It should be kept cold during the preparation to avoid curdling. It is usually served with salad but it is a delicious cold sauce with shellfish, fish, poultry and cooked vegetables, especially asparagus.

134

Numerous kinds of mayonnaise are made from a basic mayonnaise, such as **green mayonnaise** (with finely-chopped parsley, chives, sage and thyme), **curried mayonnaise** (with curry powder or paste), **tomato mayonnaise** (with tomato purée and a few drops of tabasco or worcester sauce). Sauces made from a base of mayonnaise are **tartare sauce** (with gherkins, capers, chives, French mustard and vinegar), **rémoulade sauce** (with French mustard, anchovy essence, chopped gherkins, vinegar and dry white wine) and **escoffier sauce** (with horse radish, parsley and chervil).

Associations
In France, **chantilly** or **mayonnaise chantilly** is used as a cold sauce consisting of mayonnaise to which whipped cream has been added. **Maionese** is the Italian for mayonnaise.
see: **äioli, cole slaw, dressing, fillet, mousseline, remoulade, salad, tartare, vitello tonnato**

Medallion

medallions of pork

Origin
Medal and **medallion** are derived from the French word **médaille**, which itself came from the Latin **metallum** meaning *metal.* The word describes a circular piece of metal or something with a round shape.

Meaning
A **medallion** in cuisine means a skinless, boneless round (and sometimes oval) of meat, which is usually cut from the loin of pork, lamb or veal. It is tied with a string to retain its round shape during cooking. It can be cooked in whatever way one prefers.

Associations
see: **tournedos**

Meringue

Pronounced MA-RANG (with first a as in ago and second as in sang)

Origin
Meringues have been made since the beginning of the 18th century. It is thought to have originated in Meiringen, a town in Switzerland, by a Swiss pastrycook called Gasparini in 1720. It became very popular in French court circles.

Meaning
A **meringue** is a very light, delicate foam confection made by slowly beating egg whites then adding fine caster sugar and just a dash of salt. The volume of the egg whites can be increased eightfold by beating. There should be no egg yolks or oil in the mixing bowl, as these will reduce the foam's volume. The egg whites should not be overbeaten (to avoid clumping) but should be whisked until the foam is able to stand up in clear peaks. There are two kinds of meringues: **soft meringue** which is used for the toppings of pies and puddings and **hard meringue**

which is used for meringue cases, pavlovas and meringue cakes. Soft meringues require less sugar than hard meringues. They should be baked in a moderate oven for about 15 to 20 minutes (depending upon the hardness of the meringue required) until they have a light, golden exterior and soft interior. Small rosettes of meringue can be sandwiched together and filled with whipped cream. A popular meringue dish throughout the world is **lemon meringue pie**, which is a crispy pastry shell

lemon meringue pie

with a filling of lemon curd, topped with meringue. Fruit and fresh cream are perfect accompaniments to meringues, which make an excellent dessert.

Associations

Italian meringue is made by pouring warm sugar syrup onto beaten egg whites. A **vacherin** is a dessert made from the shell of a meringue which is filled with fruit and fresh cream, chantilly cream or ice cream. In French cuisine, small vacherins are called **corbeilles**. Vacherin is also cheese from Savoie (or Savoy) in the South East of France. **Floating islands** is an English dessert consisting of blobs (*islands*) of meringue floating in a sea of egg custard. **Hov dessert** is a Swedish dessert consisting of meringues with a chocolate sauce. The Portuguese enjoy meringue cookies called **suspiros**, which means *sighs*.
see: **crème, croquembouche, pavlova, soufflé, torte**

Mezze

Origin
Mezze derives from an Arabic word **mezzeh** meaning *a selection of starters to a meal.* The same word with slightly different spelling is used in Greece, Lebanon and the Near East countries to mean a snack or hors d'oeuvre.

Meaning
Mezze (Greek) and **mezeler** (Turkish) form what is known in Greek as **mezethakia** or *little appetizers,* which are very popular in cafés in Greece, Turkey; Syria, Lebanon, Palestine and the Balkan areas. The savoury appetizers consist of a wide and varied range of small dishes, such as dips, like **taramasalata, hummus** and **tzatziki** (made with chopped cucumber, garlic and yoghurt), salads, like **melitzanosalata** (made with aubergines), feta and other cheeses, grilled sardines and other small fish, garlic sausage, roasted offal, hard-boiled eggs, roasted octopus and squid, stuffed mussels, beans, salted nuts, onion rings, cucumber and **dolmades.**

Associations
see: **appetizer,   chickpeas,   dolmades,   spanikopita, taramasalata, tahini, yoghurt**

Mille feuille

Pronounced   MEEL - FUR -YEE (with ee as in see, u as in fur and ee as in see)

Origin
Mille is French for *a thousand* and **feuille** for *leaf.*

Meaning
Mille feuille is a puff pastry consisting of layers of oblong pastry laid one on top of another with cream (fresh or chantilly) and jam or a fruit purée also layered. It is usually topped with icing. It is also called a **vanilla slice**, as the chantilly cream is flavoured with vanilla.

Associations
Mille foglie (a *thousand leaves*) is the Italian for **mille feuille.**
see: **feuilltage, purée**

Minestrone

Pronounced MINA -STRONAY (with i as in pin, a as in ago, o as in over and ay as in say)

Origin
Minestrone derives from the Italian **minestrare** meaning *that which is served.* **Minestra** means *soup.* It is believed that the soup was served by monks to travellers who called at their monastery.

Meaning
Minestrone is a thick soup of various vegetables, herbs and garlic, which is thickened with rice or pasta (e.g. macaroni). There are different versions of the soup in various parts of Italy. In Genoa in Northern Italy, the Genoese add **pesto** to the soup when it is served. **Minestrone alla Milanese** has bacon and rice added to the vegetables. **Minestrone alla Fiorentina** adds **soffritto,** which is a flavouring made from pork, red chillis, chicken giblets and tomato sauce. The soup is very filling and can almost be a meal in itself.

minestrone soup

Associations
see: **pasta, pesto, rice**

Mirepoix

Pronounced MEER-PWA (with ee as in see and a as in cat)

Origin
In the 18th century in France during the reign of King Louis XV (1715-1774), it became a custom for the king to honour aristocratic members of the court by naming dishes after them. A French general, the **Duc de Mirepoix** (who died in 1757) was so honoured by having a garnish named after him.

Meaning
Mirepoix is a mixture of diced vegetables which are steamed or cooked in butter with spices. The mixture usually includes celery, onions, carrots and a bay leaf and sometimes it also has ham or lean fried bacon. It is often a foundation on which fish, shellfish and meat are braised. It is also used to flavour stews and sauces.

Associations
A **brunoise** is a garnish for soups made from mirepoix and a little butter.
see: **daube, garnish**

Mirin

Pronounced MEE-RIN (with ee as in see and i as in bin)

Origin
Mirin is Japanese for a *sweet rice wine.*

Meaning
Mirin is a sweet wine made from glutinous, short-grained rice. It has an

Photograph kindly supplied by Kikkoman Corporation

alcohol content of 13% to 22%. It is never used for drinking but is used in Japanese cooking to add a sweet and distinctive flavour to a dish, such as boiled or grilled fish. It is also used as a basting

sauce to glaze grilled food

Associations

Sake (pronounced sa-kay, with a as in far and ay as in say) is another Japanese rice wine. It is a very popular alcoholic drink in Japan, but it is also used to season cooked dishes.
see: rice, sukiyaki, sushi, tempura, teriyaki

Miso

Pronounced   MISAW (with i as in pin and aw as in saw)

Origin

Miso is a Japanese word meaning a *soya bean and salt paste.* It was introduced into Japan from China in the 7th century and became very popular in the 14th century.

Photograph from " Japanese Cooking for Health and Fitness" by Kyoko Konishi, published by Gakken & Co. Ltd.

miso soups

Meaning

Miso is a semi-solid paste which is made from steamed soya beans, salt and a fermenting agent (**kojii**) made from rice and wheat. The paste, which is eaten throughout Japan, varies from region to region, according to its salt and starch content and also whether rice, barley or wheat is added to it. There are many kinds of miso, each with its distinctive flavour, texture, colour and aroma. It is a flavour enhancer and also it is able to remove the fishiness of seafoods. It is used in Japan in most dishes (e.g. grilled, fried and preserved dishes), in marinades and dressings and even in cakes. **Miso shiru** is also a very popular soup in Japan, which, traditionally, is eaten at breakfast. To make miso soup, miso

mash is added to **dashi**. The soup can be garnished with vegetables in season, shellfish, seaweeds or one of the different kinds of **tofu**.

Associations
see: **dashi, garnish, seaweed, soya, sushi, tofu**

Morel

Pronounced   MO-REL (with o as in got and e as in bell)

Origin
Morel is from the Greek **morchel** and the French **morille** meaning an *edible fungus.* Mushrooms have been eaten throughout the world for thousands of years. The Ancient Romans were very fond of them and liked them cooked in honey. Mushrooms were first cultivated commercially in France in the 17th century.

Meaning
A **morel** is a *mushroom*, which is not a vegetable but belongs to the fungus family. It has a spongey surface and an elongated cap which resembles the cross-section of a honeycomb. It has a distinctive and delicate flavour but little perfume. Morels can be stuffed and baked or added to stews and casseroles. They are exported around the world in tins or dried and distributed in packages.

a morel

Associations
The **cèp** (or **porcino** in Italian), which looks like a glossy bun, is one of tastiest of mushrooms. It is usually sold dried and it increases its flavour when cooked. The **chanterelle** (or **girolle**) is shaped like a funnel or trumpet. It is popular for many dishes in Europe. Japan   has two main

a field mushroom

types of mushrooms in its cuisine. The first is **matsutake** o r **pine mushroom**, which is grown in pine forests. They are an expensive delicacy in Japan. The second is **shiitake** (pronounced *shee-ee-tak-ay*) which is a large,black mushroom which is used sparingly in many dishes because of its distinctive and strong flavour. The **straw mushroom** or **paddy mushroom** is a tiny, cultivated fungus in the form of a sheath with the mushroom inside. It is popular in Japan and other countries.

Mornay sauce

Pronounced MOR-NAY (with o as in more and ay as in say)

Origin
The inventor of **mornay sauce** was **Joseph Voiron,** the chef at the Restaurant Durand in Paris during the reign of Napoleon 111 (1852-1870). He named mornay sauce after **De Plessis Mornay,** a 16th century Huguenot (French Protestant), whom he admired.

Meaning
Mornay sauce consists of **béchamel sauce,** into which is stirred a combination of finely-grated cheeses, such as   gruyére and parmesan, and a little cayenne pepper or mustard. The sauce is usually served with eggs, fish, vegetables (such as cauliflower, leeks and asparagus) and gratinéed dishes (e.g. macaroni cheese).

Associations
see: **crustacean, béchamel, florentine, gratinée, parmigiano**

Mortadella

Pronounced MOR-TA-DELA (with o as in port, a's as in far and e as in tell)

Origin
There are two versions of the origin of **mortadella.** One is that it originated in monasteries in the Emilia Romagne area of Italy in the 13th century. The monks crushed pork with a pestle in a

mortar called a **mortaio della carne di maiale,** literally *a mortar for the meat of a pig.* As this was quite a mouthful to say, the phrase was shortened to **mortadella** - and what was to become a famous sausage was named. The other version is that it derives from the Latin **myrtatella,** which is the Ancient Roman description of a sausage flavoured with *myrtle berries.* As spices were brought into Europe, the myrtle was superseded by peppercorns in the sausage.

Meaning

A **mortadella** is a large, lightly-spiced, smoked sausage which is usually made from pork but occasionally from a mixture of pork and beef. Sometimes it is studded with pistaschio nuts. It is a speciality of the city of Bologna in Northern Italy. It is made using a fermentation and dehydration process to ensure that it preserves well. It requires no refrigeration or cooking before it can be eaten. Usually it is cut into paper-thin slices and is often served as part of antipasto.

Associations

see: **antipasto, hors d'oeuvre, sausage, wurst**

Moussaka

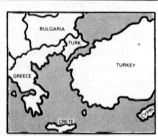

Pronounced MOO-SAKA (with oo as in soon, and a's as in cat)

Origin

Moussaka is a Greek word which originated from the Arabic **musakk'a.** It became **musaca** in Rumania and **musaka** in Bulgaria. It is best known as a Greek or Turkish dish, where it is very popular. It is eaten throughout the Balkans and the Middle East, where **aubergines** grow in profusion. **Aubergine** derives from the Persian word **badindjan.** The Arabs put **al** (meaning *the*) in front of it and called it **al-badindjan.** Europeans simplified the word and it became **aubergine.**

Meaning

Moussaka consists of alternate layers of peeled, sliced and chopped **aubergines** (also called **eggplant**) which have been cooked in oil and layers of minced meat (usually lamb or mutton). The final layer (which sometimes comprises sauteed mushrooms, tomatoes and onions) is usually covered with a cheese-custard sauce made with eggs, milk, flour, grated cheese, nutmeg and seasoning. The dish is gratinéed until it is golden brown. An attractive entrée is a hollowed-out aubergine filled with moussaka.

Associations
see: entrée, gratinée

Mousse

mango mousse

Pronounced MOOS (with oo as in soon)

Origin
Mousse derives from the Latin **mulsa** meaning a mixture of honey and water (called a hydromel) and also the French **mousse** meaning a *froth* or *foam*. The name was used in the 18th century to describe a very light, frothy dessert.

Meaning

There are many different kinds of **mousses**. Not all of them now have the frothy, creamy texture of the original mousses. Some are now more like a jelly in texture. They usually consist of puréed fruit, caster sugar, water, eggs, double cream, perhaps a liqueur and gelatine to ensure that they set. They are often garnished with chopped nuts, glazed fruit or flaked chocolate. They are usually served cold and more often than not they are made in a mould or served in individual glasses or coupes.

Associations

Chocolate mousse is one of the most popular desserts in the Western world. Although it is usually associated with French cuisine, it originated in Spain. The Italian for mousse is **spuma** or **sfomato**. A **délice** is chocolate (white or dark) mixed with cream, which is made in a mould in a mousse form. Nowadays, there are also various savoury mousses.
see: **crème, dessert**

Mousseline

Pronounced MOOSA-LEEN (with oo as in soon, a as in ago and ee as in see)

Origin

Mousseline is derived from the material called **mousseline,** which itself comes from the word **muslin,** a plain-weave, cotton fabric. The mousseline material had on its surface many small puffs which made it look rather like moss. The French for *moss* is **mousse**. The term was probably used in cuisine because the surface of the dish appeared to have small, moss-like patterns.

Meaning

A **mousseline** is a very light dish of puréed fish (less often of chicken or veal) to which egg white or cream has been added. It refers, too, to hollandaise sauce or to mayonnaise to which whipped cream, eggs, and grated nutmeg have been added, or to any preparations (particularly pastes) to which whipped cream has been added to enrich them.

Associations

see: **crème, hollandaise, mayonnaise, purée**

146

Mulligatawny

Pronounced
MULYGA-TAWNY (with u as in mutton, y's as in duty, a as in ago and aw as in saw)

Origin
Mulligatawny derives from the Tamil (Indian) words **mullaga** meaning *black pepper* and **tanni** meaning *water* or *broth.* Literally it means *black pepper water.*

Meaning
Mulligatawny is a soup made from beef, chicken or fish stock. Vegetables are added and it is spiced with curry. It can be served thick or thin, depending upon the amount of vegetables used.

Associations
see: **curry, stock**

Naan

Pronounced
NAN (with a as in far)

Origin
Naan is a Hindi word meaning a type of *leavened bread.*

Meaning
Naan (also spelled **nan**) is a flat, leavened bread made from a dough of white flour, yeast, yoghurt, water, a little sugar, salt and ghee. Sometimes eggs are added. Traditionally, it is cooked in the Punjab in India and in Pakistan in a tandoor oven. The dough is stuck to the sides of the oven while a chicken is cooked inside the oven on a spit. The bread is shaped like a teardrop and it is of a size made for individuals rather than for a group of people. It is often sprinkled with poppy seeds. It is served with almost all Indian meat and vegetable dishes, such as kebabs, korma and tandoori chicken.

Associations
see: **ghee, kebab, korma, yoghurt, tandoori**

Nasi goreng

Pronounced NASEE GORENG (with a as in far, ee as in see , o as in pot, e as in pet and final g as in cognac).

Origin
Nasi is Malay for cooked *rice* and **goreng** for *fried*. **Nasi goreng** is literally *fried rice.* Indonesian and Malay food which originated in **Padang** in Sumatra is known as **nasi Padang**.

nasi goreng

Meaning
Nasi goreng, which is a very popular dish in Malaysia and Indonesia, is made from cooked rice, shredded omelette, onions, oil, **blachan**, chopped chicken meat and prawns. The rice mixture is fried and coconut milk is added. The dish is garnished with omelette shreds or onion flakes and is served with prawn crackers, called **krupuk**.

148

Associations

Blachan is the most popular flavouring in Malaysian and Indonesian cuisine. It consists of a paste made from pounded prawns, sardines (or other very small fish) and chillies which is fermented and then mashed with salt. **Nasi goreng** or **fried rice** is cooked in a large, open pan called a **kuali** in Malaya, a **wok** in China and a **wajan** in Indonesia.

see: **chilli, garnish, rice**

Navarin

Pronounced
NAVA-RA (with the first two a's as in cat and the final a as in a naselised a in sang)

Origin
Navarin is French for mutton stew. The name was coined by the famous French chef and writer Antonin Carême in 1830. The name was used to celebrate the defeat of the Turkish and Egyptian navies at Navarino (off the south coast of Greece) by the combined fleets of France and Russia in 1827.

Meaning
A **navarin** is a ragoût or stew exclusively of mutton, or less often, of lamb. The meat is casseroled with small onions, potatoes and turnips and sometimes with one or two other vegetables as a garnish.

Associations
see: **bonne femme, casserole, garnish, ragoût**

Noisette

Pronounced
NWA-ZET (with a as in cat and e as in pet)

Origin
In French, **noisette** is a small version of **noix**, which means a *walnut*. The **noix** of a leg of lamb or ham means a small, walnut-shaped (roughly round) and nut-sized piece, which is a juicy morsel.

Meaning

A **noisette** is a small, round or oval slice of lamb or mutton which is cut from the leg, rib or fillet. It is cut to provide an individual portion. It usually weighs about 70 to 90 grams and is no less than 1.25 cms thick. To make a noisette, the bone is

beef noisettes with prunes

removed from the meat and the "tail" of the piece is wrapped around the centre piece to form a circle of meat. It is usually secured with a small skewer. The meat is usually sautéed, either plain or crumbed, in butter and is frequently served on a croûton. The term is also used to describe a slice of veal or beef fillet. **Noisette** also describes potatoes which have been shaped into small balls.

Associations

see: croûte, fillet, pomme

Noodles

Pronounced NOO-DALS (with oo as in soon and a as in ago)

Origin
Noodles, as a simple pasta dish made from grain, have been eaten by people throughout the world for thousands of years. They have been a basic dish in the diets of countries as far from each other as China and Italy. The *word* **noodle** derives from the German **nudel.**

Meaning
A **noodle** is a pasta made from a dough consisting of flour, water and eggs. The noodles from China, Japan, Java, Indonesia and Malaya are plainer and finer than those from European countries such as Italy, Germany and Hungary. Noodles can be served fresh and hot in melted butter or *au gratin* as a separate course, served with a main dish, or be added to soups in a dry form.

noodles

Associations

Wan tons (also spelled **won-ton**) or, as they are sometimes called, **Chinese ravioli** or **cloud swallows** are very thin, square sheets of dried noodles, which are made from wheat flour, eggs, water and seasoning. The dough is used to make packages for savoury mixtures, rather like stuffed pancakes. The packages are fried steamed or boiled. Wan-tons are the main ingredient in Chinese short soup. They are also deep fried as a favourite snack in China. As the paper-thin sheets of dough are hard to make, wan tons are usually bought in packets from special food shops.

In China noodles are called **mein** (as in **chow mein**). The Japanese make noodles called **udon** from wheat flour. Another very popular noodle dish in Japan is **soba**, which is made from 80% buckwheat flour and 20% wheat flour. Noodles served in soup, probably with a savoury topping, are common luncheon snacks in Japan. **Rigatoni** are ribbon-shaped noodles which are eaten in Italy with parmesan cheese.

see: gratinée, parmigiano, pasta, sukiyaki

Oeufs en cocottes

Pronounced

URF - ON - KOKOT (with u as in fur, first o as a naselised o in song, second and third o's as in got)

Origin

Oeuf is French for *egg,* **en** for *in* and **cocotte** for a *stewing pan.*

Meaning

Oeufs en cocotte are made by lightly buttering **ramekins** then placing slices of sausage or bacon on the bottom of each. The ramekins are placed in a pan of hot water or in a bain marie and covered with foil. They are then baked for about ten minutes. The ramekins are removed and a fresh egg is broken into each one. Each is topped with cream, seasoned and then baked just until the eggs set. They are garnished with paprika and served hot.

Associations

see: **bain marie, ramekin**

Omelette

Pronounced OM -LAT (with o as in bomb and a as in ago)

Origin

There are two versions of the origin of the term **omelette**. One is that it derives from the French **amelette** (later alumette), which in turn comes from the Latin **lamella** meaning a *thin metal plate*. The second version is that it derives from the Latin **ova melita**, which means *honeyed eggs.* The Ancient Romans had no cane or beet sugar and relied on honey and grape syrup to sweeten some of their desserts. A favourite dessert with them was honeyed eggs. Omelettes have been eaten throughout the world for thousands of years.

peach soufflé omelette

Meaning

There are three basic kinds of **omelette** (also spelled **omelet**): **English** (or **soufflé**) **omelette** which is fairly thick, light and fluffy and should be eaten immediately after it is made before it deflates; **French** (or **plain**) **omelette** which is light and plump and not as dry in texture as the soufflé omelette and **Spanish** (or **tortilla**) **omelette**, which is like a thin pancake and contains vegetables. A basic omelette is made from fresh eggs, cold water or milk and a sprinkle of salt, if desired. The mixture is beaten until it is light and foamy and then poured immediately into an omelette pan, in which there is about a tablespoon of melted butter or margarine. The heat should be high. When it is cooked , the omelette should be moist but well-done and have a golden brown surface. It becomes hard if over-cooked. Various fillings can be added to the basic mixture, such as grated cheese, diced mushrooms, asparagus, spinach, bacon and parsley (or fines herbes), which are very popular savoury additions and fruit purées and jams as sweet additions.

Associations
Omelette à la Savoyarde (from the Haute Savoie district in France, near the Swiss border) consists of an omelette filled with slices of sautéed potatoes with thin slivers of tasty cheese (such as gruyère). Omelette in Indonesia is **daar**; in India it is **omlate**; in Italy it is **frittata**.
see: **crêpe, pomme, soufflé, torte, tortilla**

Osso buco

Pronounced   OSO (with o's as in got) , BOOKO (with oo as in moon and o as in go)

Origin
In Italian, **osso** means *bone* and **buco** means a *hole.* **Osso buco** literally means *a bone with a hole in it* or *a hollow bone.* It is a Milanese dish which originated in the 12th century.

Meaning
Osso buco (the plural is **ossi buchi**) is made from part of the knuckle or shank of veal with some meat still on it and the bone marrow left in. It is casserolled slowly in stock and wine with vegetables, garlic and seasoning and then it is usually served on a bed of rice (traditionally **risotto Milanese**) or on buttered

osso buco

pasta. A long-handled spoon (or an oyster fork) is used to remove the marrow from the bones - which, in fact are not hollow, as the term **osso buco** suggests.

Associations
see: casserole, risotto

Paella

Pronounced PA-EYA (with first a as in far, e as in pet , y as in yet and final a as in ago)

Origin
There are two versions of the origin of the term **paella.** One is that it derives from the large, shallow, open, two-handled iron pot in which it is cooked, called in

Spanish a **poel** or **paellaras.** In the other version, the story goes that the citizens of a small Spanish town of La Albufera near Valencia heard that the Queen of Spain would be travelling in the vicinity of their town. They decided to concoct a dish in her honour. However, they could not decide on a name for the dish. So, they called it **for her**, which in Spanish is **para ella**. With time, these words changed to one word - **paella**.

Meaning

Paella is a Spanish casserole dish which is based on rice. The dish varies in Spain from district to district, depending upon the local produce available. It usually has a hotchpotch of ingredients, including rice, meat, chicken, fish, seafood, sausages (e.g.

chorizo), beans, onions and other vegetables. Invariably, the dish contains garlic and peppers. Saffron is the traditional flavouring for paella but, as it is expensive, tumeric powder is often used as an alternative.

Associations

see: **casserole, crustacean, rice, sausage**

Panada

Pronounced PAN-ADA (with the first a as in cat, the second as in far and the last as in ago)

Origin
Panada (also called **panade**) derives from the Spanish word **pan** and the Latin **panis** which mean *bread*. It came to mean bread (and later bread and butter) boiled to a pulp and then flavoured.

Meaning
Panada has two meanings. One is a soup made of bread, stock, milk or water and butter. The other is a paste made from bread, flour paste or starches, which is used to bind croquettes or forcemeats of fish or meat.

Associations
see: **croquette, stock**

Panettone

Pronounced PANAY-TON-AY (with a as in far, ay's as in say and o as in go)

Origin
Panettone originated in Milan in Northern Italy. It probably comes from **pan de Tonio**, meaning in Italian *Tony's bread*, as it was thought that a Milanese baker called Tonio first made it some time in the 15th century. Originally, it was little more than a simple, spiced bread but it has become more elaborate with the centuries.

Meaning
Panettone is a light, egg-yellow yeast cake made with sultanas and candied fruit. It usually has a dome-shaped top. It is very popular at breakfast with coffee in parts of Italy. It is particularly popular at Christmas time throughout Italy.

Associations
see: **gâteau, kugelhopf**

Papillote

Pronounced PAPEE-YOT (with a as in bat, ee as in see and o as in got)

Origin
Papillote is French for a *twist of paper* (originally for the curling of hair), a *Christmas cracker* and a *candy wrapper.* It then came to mean buttered paper used for cooking chops. The process of enclosing raw food completely in a container of leaves or bark before it is cooked has been known for thousands of years. It was, and still is, common practice on many Pacific islands and in Greece and Turkey and Malaysia, for instance, where fish or meat are wrapped in banana, pandan or vine leaves.

Meaning
A dish which is cooked **en papillote** is one which is encased in paper or foil. Until relatively recently, only paper was used but nowadays foil is invariably the **papillote**. A dish is completely covered in greased paper or foil and then baked in an oven. This method helps to retain all the natural juices in the food being cooked.

Pappadum

Pronounced PAPA-DUM (with a's as in cat and u as in rum)

Origin
Pappadum is derived from the Tamil (Indian) **parappu adam** meaning *lentil cake.* In North India it is called a **papad**.

Meaning
Pappadums (also spelled **poppadams** and **poppadums** and in eight other ways, according to the Complete Oxford Dictionary) are made from a mixture of lentil flour, pepper and water. Very light, paper-thin discs of the mixture are immersed in very hot oil. They swell and form crunchy, crisp, peppery wafers, which are served with curries and other Indian dishes.

Associations
see: **curry, dahl**

Parantha

Pronounced PA-RAN-TA (with first a as in ago, second a as in far and final a as in ago)

Origin
Parantha derives from a Tamil word meaning *puffed up.*

Meaning
Parantha is probably the favourite bread (called **roti**) of India. It is made from unleavened, wheatmeal flour (called **atta**) and plain flour combined, salt, water and a little vegetable oil or ghee to flavour it. The batter is fried or griddled until it is flaky. It is usually made in a triangular shape. It is eaten with kebabs or other dishes. The pancake of the dough is also filled with spiced cauliflower to make **gobi parantha** or with spiced potatoes to make **ala parantha.**

Associations
see: **ghee, kebab, pomme**

Parfait

Pronounced PA-FAY (with a as in father and ay as in say)

Origin
Parfait is French for *perfect.* Originally, the word referred to an ice sweet which was flavoured with coffee only.

Meaning
A **parfait** is a rich, frozen dessert made from egg whites or gelatine (to act as a setting agent), whipped cream, sugar, lemon juice, a pinch of salt and flavouring (e.g. fresh strawberries). It is usually made in a plain mould or coupe, often with different layers, and unlike a **bombe** is not enclosed in a water ice or ice cream. It is like an ice cream but has crystals, which result from its fast freezing without being stirred. Nowadays, parfait are very similar to flavoured ice creams, of which there is a very large variety. They are served as snacks or desserts.

Associations
see: **bombe, dessert**

Parmigiano

Pronounced PA-MEE-JANO (with first a as in cat, ee as in see, second a as in father and o as in go)

Origin
Parmigiano is Italian for *Parmesan cheese,* which was produced in Parma in the Emilia-Romagna region of Northern Italy more than a thousand years ago.

Meaning
Parmigiano, or **parmesan cheese**, is a rock-hard cheese, which is produced in Italy under carefully-controlled conditions only between 15 April and 11 November. It is then matured for 2 to 4 years. Nowadays, the cheese is produced not only in Italy but in many countries. It is usually grated before it is used

cannelloni with parmesan cheese

which is mainly to flavour or bring out the flavour of dishes on which it is sprinkled (e.g. on spaghetti bolognese).

Associations

À la parmesane in French cuisine means any dish which includes parmesan cheese.

see: bolognese, fetuccine, mornay sauce, noodles, pesto, pipérade, ravioli

---

Pasta

Pronounced   PASTA (with the first a as in far and the second as in ago)

Origin

Pasta derives from the Latin **pasta** meaning a **paste** or **dough**. It is Italian for **paste**, which is a dough, basically of flour and water. Originally it was called **macaroni** (which is the generic term for all pasta) and it probably was first made in Sicily. Evidence from the ruins at Pompeii shows that the Ancient

a variety of pasta

Romans were using equipment for making leganum, a kind of tagliatelli. There is reference to the use of the dish in Italian writings of the 10th century. This contradicts the claim sometimes made that Marco Polo, an Italian adventurer, brought the dish back to Italy from China in 1295. Certainly, pasta was being made in Italy in the 13th century and by the 15th century it was the mainstay of the Italian diet. There has always been a difference in the pasta of the north and south of Italy. In the more prosperous north, butter is used for cooking and flat noodles made with eggs are most common. In the less prosperous south, olive oil is used for cooking and dried, tubular pasta, like spaghetti and macaroni, are common.

Meaning

Pasta is made from the middlings of hard wheat. The wheat that is best to use is **durum** and the paste produced is sometimes enriched by the addition of eggs. In Italy alone, there are at least

70 different kinds of pasta (there are many more throughout the world), each with a name which describes its shape, its origins or the fillings it usually has, such as **agnolotti** ("*fat little lamb*"), **cannelloni** ("*big pipes*"), **vermicelli** ("*little worms* "), **spaghetti** ("*little strings* "), **lasagne** ("*broad leafed* "). The pastas have four basic shapes: cords, tubes, ribbons and special shapes, such as shells, butterflies and crests. Probably the best known pastas outside Italy are **spaghetti, macaroni, cannelloni, fettucine** and **lasagne.** In Italy, a number of soups contain pasta and each can constitute a meal in itself. The range of sauces which accompany pastas is very wide. Certainly one of the most popular in Italy is **pommarola,** a rich tomato sauce.

Associations
At Pontedassio, south west of Genoa in Northern Italy, is situated a **Museum of Spaghetti.**
see: **al dente, bolognese, fettucine, lasagne, macaroni, minestrone, noodles, pasty, pesto, ravioli, semolina, spaghetti**

Pasty

Cornish pasties

Pronounced   PASTY (with a as in cat or far and y as in duty)

Origin

Pasty derives from the Old English and Old French word **pastee**, which comes from the Latin **pasta** meaning *paste* or dough. Originally, the pasty crust was made not to be eaten but to protect the ingredients inside the pastry from flies and insects and also from the fierce heat of ovens.

Probably the best-known pasty is the **Cornish pasty** from Cornwall in the South West of England. They were said to have been produced because Cornish fishermen, some of whom were involved in smuggling, needed a good meal of meat and vegetables to sustain them while they were out in a cold sea, usually in situations where they could not do even simple cooking. The meat and vegetables they enjoyed were carried in a "package" of pastry. Some of the pasties were large and had a savoury filling at one end and a sweet (such as jam) at the other. The pastry was thick and folded and crimped to form handles so that the fishermen could hold the pasty without dirtying most of it while eating.

Meaning

A **pasty** is made from short crust pastry and can be filled with just meat, just vegetables (such as diced potatoes, carrots, turnips and chopped onions or any other vegetables in season) or both meat and vegetables, with seasoning and a little parsley. Cooked fruit, such as apple, or purées or conserves can also be used to make sweet pasties.

Associations

A **turnover** is a semi-circular pasty made by folding a circle of pastry dough in half and sealing the edges. It usually has a sweet filling, such as cooked fruit. A popular savoury pasty in Russia is the **pozharske**.

see: pasta, purée

Pâte

Pronounced PAT (with a as in tart)

Origin
Pâte is French for *paste* or *dough*, as in **pâte à pain** meaning *bread dough.*

Meaning
A **pâte** should not be confused with a **pâté**. In English, the pâtes are known as **filo pastry, puff pastry, choux pastry, short crust pastry** and **sheet pastry**. In French cuisine, a finer distinction is made among pâtes. It has **pâte à feuilletage** (puff pastry for pies, gâteaux and pastry cases), **pâte à foncer, frisée** or **brisée** (short pastry for tarts, pie crust), **pâte à sucrée** (sweet paste for flans and tarts), **pâte sablée** (with a buttery,crunchy texture which is ideal for petit four), **pâte dumpling** (sweet paste for rolls and dumplings and puddings), **pâte à choux** (choux pastry for profiteroles, éclairs and gâteaux), **pâte baba or savarin, pâte brioche, pâte frire** or **beignet** (for batter for fritters), **pâte genoise** (for sponge cake mixes and gâteaux) and **pâte crêpe** (for pancakes).

Associations
see: **choux, baba, beignet, brioche, crêpe, dumpling, éclair, feuilletage, filo, gâteau, savarin, pâté**

Pâté

Pronounced PATAY (with a as in cat and ay as in say)

Origin
Pâté was originally French for a *meat or fish pie.*

Meaning
The term **pâté** outside of France means a meat, game or fish dish with a paste consistency, which is cooked and served in an earthenware dish called a **terrine**. The pâté itself is also called a **terrine**. It is served cold, usually on toast as a snack or as an

hors d'oeuvre. Probably the most famous and best-known pâté is **pâté de foie gras**. In France, pâté has three meanings. The first is a pastry case filled with meat, fish or vegetables, which is baked in an oven and served cold. The second is **pâté en terrine** (as described above) and the third is **pâté en croûte,** which is a rich fish, game or meat mixture cooked in a pastry crust.

Associations
see: croûte, fleuron, foie gras, hors d'oeuvre, sweetbread, terrine , truffle

---

Paupiette

Pronounced   PAUP-YET (with au as in daub and e as in pet)

Origin
Paupiette is French for a *meat olive* (as in *beef olive*). The

word olive was probably used to describe the meat dish, as originally it was olive shaped

Meaning
Paupiettes are fillets of fish or thin, pounded slices of meat (usually beef or veal), which have been stuffed with a forcemeat or topped with slices of pork sausage and then rolled into a large cork or a barrel shape and wrapped and tied with a rasher of bacon. They are then braised in a stock of chopped onions, butter, sieved tomatoes, a bouquet garni and seasoning. It is very similar to a **ballotine**. The paupiettes are served with a risotto or with mixed vegetables.

Associations
A **paupiette** is also called a **beef olive** or a **roulade**. In Argentina, it is called a **matambre**, which means *kills hunger*.
see: ballotine, bouquet garni, fillet, risotto, roulade, stock

---

Pavlova

Pronounced   PAV-LO-VA
(with first a as in cat, o as in over and final a as in ago)

Origin
The pavlova was invented by Bert Sachse who was a cook in the Royal Australian Air Force. He named the light and airy dessert after the famous Russian ballerina, Anna Pavlova, whom he saw perform in Perth in Western Australia in the 1900's.

Meaning
A **pavlova** is a dish of egg whites with a pinch of salt which is beaten with caster sugar in a glass, pottery or metal bowl until it is of a stiff consistency. Granulated sugar is added a little at a time and, still beating, a little cornflour (cornstarch), a drop of vinegar or lemon juice and vanilla essence are added. The mixture is cooked in a tin at a low heat for about an hour. The

classical pavlova

meringue should have crisp shell and a soft, marshmallow centre. The shells or layers can be filled with various fillings, such as chestnut cream, bavarian cream, chocolate custard, lemon or mocha chiffon, strawberries or passion fruit, Chinese gooseberries (Kiwi fruit) or mixed fresh or canned fruit. It is usually accompanied by fresh cream or whipped cream.

Associations
see: crème, dessert

Pêche Melba

Pronounced
PASH - MELBA (with a as in parent, e as in melon and final a as in ago)

Origin
Pêche Melba was a dish invented by the world-renowned French chef and writer on cuisine, **Auguste Escoffier.** He

invented it while he was working at the Savoy Hotel in London to honour the famous Australian coloratura soprano, **Dame Nellie Melba** (1861-1931)

Meaning
Pêche Melba (or **P e a c h Melba**) consists of peaches on vanilla ice cream with the peaches covered by a raspberry purée. Escoffier's original creation had the dish served beween the wings of a swan carved out of ice and covered with sugar.

a peach melba tartlet

Associations
Escoffier also invented **melba toast**, which is very thin bread toasted on both sides.

Pesto

Pronounced   PAY-STO (with ay as in say and o as in go)

Origin
Pesto is Italian for a *pestle*. The dish pesto was so called because the paste made was produced by crushing the ingredients in a mortar with a pestle. The dish originated in Genoa in the North of Italy, where basil, the herb essential in pesto, grows in abundance.

Meaning
Pesto is a paste consisting of parmesan cheese, sweet basil, pinenuts (and sometimes walnuts) and garlic, which is smoothed out with a little olive oil. The result is a sharp, pungent, aromatic sauce, which is served with pasta, vegetables or soup.

Pesto bread is made from a sweet dough to which basil, garlic, parsley and olive oil are added. Fingers of cheese are placed on the dough which is rolled up and then sprinkled with poppy seeds before it is baked.

Associations
see: minestrone, pasta

Petit fours

Pronounced PETEE FAU (with e as in pet, ee as in see and au as in daub)

Origin
In French, **petit** means *little* and **four** means a *baker's oven*. The **petit four** (literally the *little oven*) was usually a slower cooking oven than the large bread oven and was ideal for baking little cakes and fancy biscuits. As has happened so often in cuisine, the product has taken its name from the equipment used.

Meaning
Petit four are small, fancy biscuits (cookies) and small cakes which are often iced or glazed with coloured icing and decorated with crystallised fruit, angelica or almonds. They are often served with coffe or tea , as a snack or at the end of a formal meal.

making almond petit fours

Associations
A **colette** is a chocolate petit four. A **langue de chat** is a thin flat biscuit (cookie), like a cat's tongue, which is served as a petit four.
see: choux

Pièce de résistance

Pronounced PEE-ES DA RAY-ZIST-ANS (with ee as in see, e as in pen, a as in ago, ay as in say, i as in mist and final a as in a naselised a in sang)

Origin
Pièce is French for a *whole piece* and **résistance** means *strength.* **Pièce de résistance** in cuisine originally meant the solid food and the backbone of the meal, usually the main meat and vegetable dishes.

Meaning
A **pièce de résistence** is the *principal dish* and the *main feature* of a meal. It is also a chef's *most distinguished creation.* Another similar phrase is **tour de force**, which means a *feat of strength* or *ability.*
see: **cuisine, restaurant**

Pikelet

Pronounced PI-KLAT (with i as in mine and a as in ago)

Origin
Pikelet derives from the Old Welsh word **bara** meaning bread and **pyglyd** meaning *black.* Originally the bread was grilled and was brown or black. Pikelet became the name in the West of England and Wales for a small, round teacake, especially one which had minute holes in it, which helped butter to be absorbed.

Meaning
A **pikelet** is made from a batter which is thicker than that for pancakes or crêpes. It consists of self-raising flour, milk, a drop of vinegar, butter, a pinch of bicarbonate of soda (baking soda) and salt. The batter should be smooth and dropped by the spoonful into a griddle or a heavy frying pan (skillet) in a little hot oil or fat. It is cooked on both sides. Additional ingredients

pikelets with cream

may be added, such as yoghurt, cream or orange juice and rind. A **waffle** is similar except that it has more eggs in the batter and is cooked using a **waffle iron**. Pikelets and waffles are eaten hot with butter and perhaps conserves.

Associations
Other breadcakes very similar to the pikelet are the **scottish pancake**, a **girdle** or **griddle cake**, a **drop scone** and a **crumpet**.

see: **crème, crêpe, yoghurt**

Pilaf

Pronounced   PIL-AF (with i as
in fill and a as in cat)

Origin
Pilaf derives from the Persian (now Iranian) word **pilaw** meaning a *rice dish*. **Pilaf** (also called **pilaff, pilau, pilav** and **palov**) is a method of preparing rice which originated thousands of years ago in the Middle East. It is a common and popular dish in Greece, Turkey, India, Indonesia, Malaysia and all Middle East countries.

Meaning

pilaf and lamb

Pilaf is made from rice (Indian long-grained **barmati** rice is ideal for it.), which is first browned in butter and then cooked in seasoned stock (e.g. chicken stock) in a tightly-covered pot until all the stock is absorbed by the rice. It may then be added to one of: fish, shellfish, poultry, offal, meat, or vegetables. Spices are then added. Other ingredients which are included in the various versions of pilaf are fried, chopped onions, chopped peppers, tomatoes, raisins, lemon juice and boiling water. The mixture is casseroled until the rice has absorbed the liquid. A traditional accompaniment to the pilaf is a sauce of melted butter with raisins and blanched, slivered almonds.

Associations

see: **almond, casserole, crustacean, rice, risotto, stock**

Pipérade

Pronounced   PEEP-ERAD
(with ee as in see, e as in pet and a as in cat or, alternatively as in made)

Origin
Pipérade derives from the Sanskrit **pippala** and the Latin **piper**, which mean*pepper*. The dish originated in the Basque Provinces of Northern Spain.

Meaning
A **pipérade** is a dish consisting of olive oil, chopped onions, tomatoes, garlic, seasoning, chopped basil and, most importantly, green peppers. Eggs, one by one, are added to the mixture which is whisked to obtain a fluffy, light texture . It is usually served with gammon and eggs and sometimes a garnish of croûtons and grated parmesan cheese.

Associations
see: **croûte,   gammon, parmigiano, purée**

Pithiviers

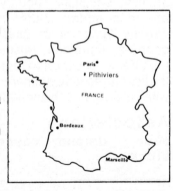

Pronounced   PEETEE-VYA (with
ee's as in see and a as in say)

Origin
The pithivier was first made in a small village called Pithiviers, which is situated in the area of Loiret in Central France.

Meaning
A **pithivier** is a round, flat cake which has layers of light puff pastry. Traditionally, it is filled with almond cream but it may also be filled with chopped almonds and crème pattissière flavoured with cointreau.

Associations
see: almond, crème, feuilletage

Pizza

Pronounced PEETZA (with ee as in see and a as in ago)

Origin

Pizza was originally an Italian word to describe any *pie* or *cake.* The flan as we know it originated from the left-over bits of dough that cooks had after they had made bread. Pizzas became very popular with the arrival of tomatoes in Italy from Mexico and South America in the 16th century. Other ingredients were added, such as **mozzarella cheese** (which melts very easily), and it became a dish not only of the general population but also of kings, such as the Bourbons, a family of French origin which occupied the thrones of France, Naples and Spain for generations.

Meaning

A **pizza** is a round, flat **flan**, varying in size from small invidual pizzas to large pizzas for groups of people. The pastry base, which is made from a dough similar to that used for scones and some breads, can vary in thickness and texture. It is covered with either one filling (such as cheese) or a medley of ingredients, such as tomatoes, cheese, anchovies, olives, sliced sausage and much more. Spices are added to the toppings and oregano in particular has traditionally been used in the making of pizzas. There are now hundreds of different recipes for pizza throughout the world.

Associations

Miniature pizzas are called **pizzettes** and a **pizzeria** is where pizzas are made. A **pissaldiere**, a speciality of Nice in France, is a savoury tart resembling a pizza but it is made with pastry which is lighter and drier than that for pizza. It can be made with or without tomatoes and is generally served as an entrée but it can also be a main dish with salad. The **Pizza di Sposa** (or *marriage pizza*) recalls that originally pizza also referred to a cake in Italy. It is a layered sponge cake with a chocolate and liqueur flavouring.

see: **entrée, fan, flan, scone, tart**

Polenta

Pronounced PO-LEN-TA (with o as in go, e as in lend and a as in far)

Origin

Polenta is from the Latin **pulentum,** which meant *grain*. The Ancient Romans used grain which they made into porridge, gruel or a type of scone as their staple food. Soldiers of the Roman Empire carried the grain in bags into many countries. The grain at that time was millet or spelt (a very coarse wheat) and later barley. Today, polenta is made from maize or Indian corn (corn meal) which makes it much finer than the grain used in former times. The dish polenta was introduced into the port of Venice in North Italy by traders from Turkey.

Meaning

Polenta is a porridge which is usually made from yellow corn meal (maize) but it can be made from semolina and even chestnut flour. To the flour is added salt and it is cooked first (It may be recooked.) in boiling water- traditionally in Italy in a special copper pot. Often the porridge-like dough is made into scones or cakes. The cooked polenta can be fried in oil or baked and served with a sauce or it can be enriched with butter or cheese. Slices of polenta are served as an accompaniment to many kinds of   savoury dishes. It is a staple food in Northern Italy and in other parts of Europe.

Associations
see: **gnocchi, marron, semolina**

Pomme (de terre)

Pronounced   POM (with o as in got)

Origin
Pomme is the French for *apple* but in many recipes and on most restaurants' menus it is an abbreviation for **pommes de terre** (literally *apples of the earth*), which is French for *potato.* The potato was brought into Spain from Quito in Equador in South America in the early 16th century. A member of Sir Walter Raleigh's second expedition to Virginia in the New World (U.S.A.) at the end of the 16th century is thought to have introduced the potato plant to England, but potatoes did not become popular as a food   until 200 years later and even then there was some suspicion by some about   its suitability as a food.

Meaning
Pommes frites, meaning literally *fried potatoes,* is probably one of the best-known terms in international cuisine. In the U.S.A. and increasingly in other countries, they are called **French fries. Chips,** another name for pommes frites, were invented not as one might think by the French but by the Belgians, who, traditionally, garnish their chips with mayonaisse. Mashed potatoes, another common and popular dish throughout the world, are called **purée de pommes** on French menus and **pommes sautée** are potatoes sautéed in butter. There are more than 30 ways of preparing potatoes. For example, **pommes allumettes** are **matchstick potatoes, pommes soufflées** are puffed, deep-fried oval potato slices; **pommes pailles** or **straw potatoes** are the thinnest and

narrowest possible strips of potato; **pommes gaufrettes** are thin, waffle-shape, deep-fried potato slices. One of the most famous of potato dishes is **pommes Dauphine** (from the Dauphine area of France) . It consists of boudins or croissants of mashed potatoes mixed with choux pastry (without sugar) which are fried in fat. **Duchesse potatoes** is a dish consisting of mashed potatoes mixed with egg yolks. The potatoes are usually piped into a pyramid shape. They form an elegant and attractive garnish to many dishes. Bavaria in South Germany has a famous dish called **Himmel und Erde** (literally *heaven and earth*) which consists of mashed potatoes cooked with apples and blutwurst, a kind of black pudding.

Associations
In France or in French restaurants, a dish which is **parmentier** means *with potatoes.* The term originated with the French gourmet Antoine-Auguste Parmentier, who introduced the potato to France in 1786. In French cuisine, **omelette parmentier** is an omelette with slices of potato in it. **Hachis parmentier** is **shepherd's pie.**
see: **bonne femme, croissant, garnish, gourmet, maître d'hôtel, noisette, omelette, parantha, sauerbrauten purée, soufflé, wurst**

Pot au feu

Pronounced
PO-TAU-FUR (with o as in go, au as in daub and u as in fur)

Origin
Pot au feu is French for *pot (or pan) on the fire.* It has been a traditional dish in France for centuries. The phrase refers also to a large casserole pan.

Meaning
Pot au feu in France refers to a simple casserole dish of meat or a combination of meats and common vegetables (such as potatoes, carrots, onions, leeks), which is seasoned with local herbs and then simmered slowly for hours in a casserole (or marmite). Sometimes the broth from the casserole is seasoned with cloves and served as a soup.

Poularde

Pronounced POO-LARD (with oo as in soon and a as in cat)

Origin
A **poularde** in French cuisine is a *fattened hen* or *roasting chicken.*

roast chicken with grapefruit segments

Meaning
A simple **chicken in a pot** dish in France can be called a **poularde à la bonne femme, poularde à la finacière** or **poularde en cocotte.** French cuisine has a variety of names for chicken. A **poussin** is a *chick* or *Spring chicken.* A **poulet** also means a chicken or fowl, as in **poulet chasseur** (chicken with tomatoes and spices). Tarragon is a favourite herb with the French when cooking chicken and **poulet l'estragon**

(chicken with tarragon) is very popular. A **poule** is a *hen* as in **poule au pot** which is *chicken broth.* A **coq** is a *cock bird* , as in **coq au vin,** the famous dish where chicken is casserolled in red wine. A **capon** is a young castrated and fattened cock bird. The word **volaille** is used as a general term for *poultry* or *fowls.* A famous international dish, which originated in Russia, is **chicken Kiev,** which takes its name from the city of Kiev in the Ukraine in the U.S.S.R. Chicken breasts are wrapped around solid segments of butter and then coated with bread crumbs. The fillets are fried in fat until golden brown. When the chicken pieces are pierced, they release a jet of butter.

Associations
À la reine (which literally means *in queenly style*) is a term in French cuisine which means *with chicken,,* for example **consommé à la reine** and **vol au vent à la reine.**
see: **bonne femme, consommè, coq au vin, marengo, suprême, vol au vent**

Profiterole

Pronounced   PROFIT-AROL (with first o as in go, i as in bit, a as in ago and the final o as in got)

Origin
Profiterole derives from the French **profiter** meaning *to profit, benefit* or *gain* and the suffix **erole**, which means *small.* It literally means *a little profit* - a little something to one's advantage. It was applied to the cake to indicate that one would benefit from the small pleasure it would give. When they were first made is not known but they were being made in the 16th century.

Meaning
Profiteroles are small balls of choux pastry which are baked in a moderate oven until they are crispy and then filled with a savoury (e.g. purèes of chicken, game or meat or cheese mixtures) or sweet mixture (e.g. creams, custards or jams). The filling is piped into the puffs through a forcing bag. Savoury profiteroles can be used as a garnish for soups and sweet profiteroles are used for making croquembouche and some gâteaux. They make an excellent, light dessert.

Associations
Italian profiteroles are called **sfinci di san Giuseppe** (*Saint Joseph Day pastries*). They are filled with custard and covered with melted chocolate.
see: choux, croquembouche, dessert, feuilletage

Prosciutto

Pronounced   PRO-SHOO-TO (with the first o as in got, oo as in soon and the final o as in go)

Origin
Prosciutto   is the Italian for *h a m .* Traditionally for centuries, Italians have started a meal with something light and fresh, such as fruit. This led to the custom of having an hors d'oeuvre or an antipasto such as **prosciutto** with fruit, such as figs.

Meaning

Italy, like Germany, is famous for the quality of the hams it cures. One of the best is the air-dried ham of the Parma region in Northern Italy, especially in the small town of Langhirano, where the air is said to be the best there is for curing hams. **Prosciutto di Parma** is a pale red, dried ham that is often included in antipasto. Paper-thin slices of raw prosciutto with melon or figs is a very popular dish both in Italy and, increasingly, throughout the world.

Associations

The German **Westphalian ham (speck** is German for ham) is similar to **prosciutto.** This lightly-smoked, thinly-sliced ham is also eaten raw, often with **pumpernickel,** a coarse, tasty, dark bread made from rye flour. The French version of this ham is **jambon cru,** which in French means *raw ham.* **Spekeskinke,** which is ham cured in brine, is a Swedish "prosciutto".
see: **antipasto, hors d'oeuvre, saltimboca**

Purée

Pronounced PU-RAY (with u as in pure and ay as in say)

Origin

Purée is French for *mashed* as in **en purée** meaning vegetables, fruit or meat boiled to a pulp. The Ancient Romans were fond of fruit purées which they ate with fish.

Meaning

A **purée** is obtained by pounding, mashing and sieving a foodstuff (fruit, fish, meat or vegetables), usually by using an electric blender, until it has been reduced to a smooth and fairly mobile pulp. The consistency of a purée can be controlled by dilution with a liquid or by the addition of a thickening agent, such as a floury vegetable, a sauce or a starchy cereal. Purées are often thickened by the addition of pasta, rice, tapioca or pearl barley. In French cuisine, a purée is also one of the three thick soups (or **potages),** the others being **cream soup** and **velouté.**

Associations

Pommes purée in French cuisine means *mashed potatoes*.
Saint Germain is a soup made of a purée of fresh peas. Purées in India and Pakistan are called **bartha**.
see: **bisque, charlotte, fool, marron, mille feuille, mousseline, pipérade, pomme, sorbet, soubise, soufflé, tahini, timbale, velouté, vindaloo**

Quenelle

Pronounced   KWU-NEL (with u as in fudge and e as in bell)

Origin
Quenelle is French for a *ball* - of fish or forcemeat. The word is said to have come from the Old English word **knyll** meaning *to grind* or *to pound,* as fish or meat had to be pounded before it was formed into a ball shape.

Meaning
Quenelles are very light, ball-shaped or sausage-shaped dumplings made from minced fish, meat or poultry, which are bound into a paste or forcemeat with the addition of the whites of eggs, butter or cream and flour. They are poached in boiling water and then served with a cream sauce or velouté. Small quenelles are sometimes used as a garnish for savoury dishes.
A **quenelle de brochet** is a dumpling filled with a fish forcemeat and poached in a fish fumet.

Associations
see: **dumpling, garnish, tart,   velouté**

Quiche

Pronounced   KEESH (with ee as in see)

Origin
The word **quiche** is a French adaptation of the Alsatian-German **küche** meaning *cake.* The **quiche** was first made in Lorraine

a province in the East of France. The dish, which was originally a custard flavoured with bacon, has been eaten in the Alsace Lorraine region of France for centuries.

Meaning

A **quiche** is an open **tart** or **flan** of short-crust pastry made in a fluted flan ring or a sandwich tin. A metal base produces a crisper pastry base than does a porcelain base. It is filled with an egg and cream or milk mixture which is flavoured with a savoury ingredient (such as onion, seafood, asparagus, spinach or sweet corn). Nowadays, there is an enormous number of variations on the original theme. The best-known quiche is **quiche Lorraine**, which consists of a short-crust pastry flan the bottom of which is filled with lightly-fried bacon. It is covered with a well-beaten mixture of eggs, diced spring onions, fresh cream and seasoning. This is topped with pieces of butter. The flan is baked for about half an hour and served hot or cold. Sometimes the dish has cheese added to it. **Onion quiche**, the top of which is garnished with fillets of anchovy, is popular in France.

Associations
A German version of the quiche is the **zweielkuchen,** which is an open tart filled with onions, bacon and cream.

see: **crème, flan, fillet, hors d'oeuvre, ramekin, tart**

Raclette

Pronounced RA-KLET (with a as in bat and e as in let)

Origin
Raclette is a French word for *a scraper.* The dish **raclette** is a speciality of the canton (Swiss name for a region) of Valais in the South West of Switzerland.

Meaning
A **raclette** is like a **fondue.** The dish is made by holding a large portion of cheese close to heat (of a fire or grill). As the cheese melts, slivers of the cheese are scraped off with an implement called a **raclette.** Cheeses which melt smoothly and do not string (as mozzarella does) should be used, such as Swiss-made raclette (the name of a cheese) gruyère, Samsoe and Swiss. The cheese scrapings are eaten with potatoes cooked in their jackets or crusty French bread and with garnishes, such as marinated onions and pickles. In some restaurants, individual grills are placed on tables, so that guests may themselves scrape off their slivers of cheese .

Associations
see: **fondue, garnish**

Ragoût

Pronounced RA-GOO (with a as in rag and oo as in soon)

Origin
Ragoût derives from the French **goût** meaning *taste* and **re** meaning *again*. Literally, it means *to taste again* and came to mean *to revive one's taste* or *restore one's appetite*. It was then

applied to a simple but tasty dish which made one want to eat.

Meaning
A **ragoût** is a simple form of **stew** or **casserole**. It is made by either browning or cooking small, seasoned pieces of meat or poultry and adding a roux and stock, meat juices or water. Sometimes vegetables are included. Another **ragoût** is produced by cooking meat with potatoes as a thickener (as in **Irish stew**).

Associations
En **ragoût** in French cuiusine means *stewed*. The Italian for ragoût is **ragu** or **stufata** and in Russian it is **jarkoë**. A Malaysian beef stew similar to a ragoût is a **redang**.
see: **blanquette, bolognese, casserole, fricassée, navarin, roux, salmis, timbale**

Ramekin

Pronounced
RAMA- KIN (with first a as in lamb, second a as in ago and i as in pin)

Origin
Ramekin derives from the German **ram** meaning *cheese* and the Old German **ramkin** meaning *a cheese cake,* which was often made as an individual serving in a small pot. From this originated **ramekin** (**ramequin** in French and **rammeken** in Flemish) to describe *a small, earthenware dish.*

Meaning
Small baking dishes which are used for individual portions of any food, are called **ramekins**. The term also describes tarts made of cheese-flavoured choux pastry and tarts filled with creamed cheese. **Ramequins** are cheese fritters or small fondues which are served in pastry cases.

Associations
see: **choux, flan, fondue, oeuf en cocotte, quiche, tart**

186

Ratatouille

Pronounced RATA-TOO-EE
(with a's as in bat, oo as in soon, ee as in see)

Origin
Ratatouille derives from the French words **touiller** meaning *to stir up* and the slang word **rata** meaning a *stew*. The word is now used in France for a **stew**. It originated in the Provence region of Southern France.

Meaning
Ratatouille is a vegetable casserole made from a little oil and garlic, tomatoes, aubergines (eggplant), peppers, zucchini (courgettes), onions, seasoning and a bouquet garni. It may be served hot or cold and makes an excellent garnish to a main dish.

Associations
Rata au choux is French for *bubble-and-sqeak*.
see: **bouquet garni, casserole, réchauffé, remoulade**

Ravioli

Pronounced .RAV-EE-OLEE
(with a as in rabbit, ee's as in see and o as in go)

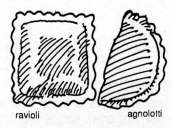

ravioli   agnolotti

Origin
Ravioli is said to have originated with **rabiole** (an Italian dialect word in the Liguria region of North Italy) meaning *things of little value* or *the left-overs.* On long journeys by ship, the sailors of the region could not waste precious food, so all the left-overs (the **rabiole**) from meals were collected, chopped up and then stuffed into little envelopes of pasta dough. They made

a filling and wholesome meal.

Meaning
Ravioli are made from small envelopes of pasta dough (made with or without eggs, according to taste), which are filled with a meat stuffing of braised veal, beef or chicken or a mixture of cream cheese, spinach and chopped egg. A common and popular meal consists of ravioli with tomato sauce and freshly-grated parmesan cheese. Ravioli are bite sized and are what the Italians call **bocconcini** meaning *little mouthfuls.*

Agnolloti is from the Italian meaning *fat little lamb,* as it was thought when the dish was first made that the pasta cases used in the dish resembed fat little lambs. It is a dish that originated in Piedmont in Northern Italy. It consists of **ravioli** made with eggs which, traditionally, are stuffed with minced meat and chopped vegetables. Nowadays, some other stuffings, such as spinach and ricotta cheese are also used. It is usually served with a sauce made of meat, melted butter and grated cheese but seafood sauce is also served when the stuffing has no meat in it.

Associations
see: **parmigiano, pasta**

Réchauffé

Pronounced
RA-SHAU-FAY (with a as in ago, au as in daub and ay as in say)

Origin
Rechauffé is French for *reheated* or *warmed up again.*

Meaning
Rechauffé is a term which describes dishes which are prepared from left-over foods from a previous meal or what the French call **debris**. A famous **rechauffé** dish is **bubble-and-squeak**, which is made from previously-cooked vegetables, such as mashed potatoes and chopped cabbage which are then fried (with or without minced or chopped meat) in oil or butter. Other dishes which can be rechauffé are shepherd's pie, cottage pie, fish cakes, hash and croquettes.

Associations
see: croquette, fricassée, ratatouille

shepherd's pie

Remoulade

Pronounced   REMOO-LAD (with e as in get, oo as in moon
and a as in add or, alternatively, as in made)

Origin
Remoulade derives from the French word **remouler** meaning
to remould or *reconstitute*.

Meaning
Remoulade is (*remoulded*) **mayonnaise** with the addition of
finely-chopped capers and chervil, anchovy essence, gherkins
and chopped dill or spring onions, parsley, mustard, perhaps a
dash of worcester sauce and chopped tarragon. Before serving,

whipped cream is sometimes added to the mixture. It is served with fish, eggs and meat.

Associations
Remouillage in French cuisine is the adding of water or more vegetables to (*remould*) a stock to make it lighter.
see: mayonnaise, ratatouille

Restaurant

Pronounced RESTO-RAUNT (with e as in best, o as in port, and au as in daub)

Origin & Meaning
Restaurant derives from the French **restaurer** meaning *to refresh, to restore (one's vigour), to set one up again.* A good hearty soup can have the effect of restoring one's energy, so *a thick soup* was called a **restaurant** in France in the 16th century. A chef by the name of Boulanger had the name **restaurant** painted over his shop to indicate that he sold soup. This attracted clients and the shop became popular and successful. Other sellers of soup and other food did the same and they, too, placed the word restaurant over their shop-front. A **restaurant** in time became a place where food was sold and eaten.
In France today, **se restaurer** means *to take refreshment* or *to feed up* (*e.g.* after illness).

Associations
Auberge, bistro, brasserie, cafateria, café, dinette, rôtisserie, tavern, taverna, all describe sit-down eating places (in contrast to *take-away food* places) which vary in comfort and quality of food. In France, a café does not usually serve meals. Restaurant is a more general word for a place to eat and implies that the quality of food, accommodation and service are good and, if the star-rating of the restaurant is high, usually of a superb standard.
see: cuisine, dégustation, maître d'hôtel, pièce de résistance

---

Rice

Pronounced   RIS (with i as in fine and s as in sweet)

Origin

The word **rice** derives from the Old French **ris**, which came
from the Latin **oryza**, which in turn probably came from the
Arabic **uruzzi** or **ruzz**. Rice has been eaten in India, China and
Japan since the beginning of recorded time. Excavation of carbon-
dated evidence shows that about 3500 B.C. it was eaten in
Thailand. It reached Europe in the 8th century when Arabs took it
to Spain. It was also brought into Europe by the Crusaders. It
became   an established and popular food in Europe in the mid
16th century.   Today, rice is the staple diet for more than half
the world's population and provides 80% of its total diet. There
are over 7000 cultivated varieties of rice in the world and India
alone grows more than 1000 varieties.

Meaning

From the many different varieties of rice, different countries (e.g. China, Japan, India, Lebanon and other Middle East countries, Italy, Spain, Mexico, Greece, Turkey) tend to favour a few of the varieties. Most Western countries and India, for instance, prefer long-grained rice and Japan and Spain favour the short-grained variety .

The grain of rice remains whole if the rice is not stirred and is cooked for only about 10 to 15 minutes. Overcooking of most rice makes it form into a thick, gluey mass. Long grained American rice is often used, as the rice grains remain separate even if the rice is overcooked. The addition of a little lemon juice or a lemon slice can enhance the colour and flavour of rice. Saffron (an expensive and almost tasteless spice) is used in many countries (e.g. India, the Middle East and Spain) to colour rice a bright yellow to make it more attractive.

Rice, which can be served boiled or fried (after boiling and drying) , is a very popular accompaniment to many savoury dishes but it is also used as a sweet (e.g. rice pudding, rice fruit flan) and as an ingredient in some desserts.

Associations

Rice in French is **riz**, in Italian **risi**, in German **reis**, in Spanish **arroz**, in **Japanese gohan** (cooked rice) and **kome** (uncooked rice), in Indian **chauval**, in malay **nasi** (cooked rice). The Chinese have a saying : "*A meal without rice is like a beautiful girl with only one eye*".

In India, **idli** are a very popular appetizer. They consist of steamed rice cakes with coconut and chutney. In Indonesia, a **rijsttafel** (literally Dutch for *a rice table*) is like a smörgåsbord but with mainly rice dishes and its accompaniments. **Nosi-maki** is a Japanese dish consisting of a bowl of rice garnished with seaweed. **Maguro-buski**, also a Japanese dish, is a bowl of steamed rice containing egg wrapped in a sliver of tuna fish or some other fish or meat. **Soubise** is a purée of onion, rice and béchamel sauce which can be used to garnish many meat dishes.

see: **curry, dessert, garnish, kedgeree, minestrone, mirin, nasi goreng, paella, pilaf, rissoto, spring rolls, sushi**

Rillette

Pronounced REE-YET (with ee as in see , y as in yes and e

as in pet)

Origin

Rillette derives from the Old French **rille** meaning *a piece of pork*. It now means a potted mince of pork or other meat, such as goose and rabbit.

Meaning

To make a **rillette**, fresh belly of pork or goose (or a combination of both) is cooked in oil or fat, then shredded into small pieces. It is then pounded into a paste consistency and seasoned. It is placed in a stone jar or earthenware pot to cool and a layer of thin lard is put on top of it to ensure it does not dry out. Like other **potted meats**, a rillette makes an excellent savoury spread on bread, toast or croûtons. It is often served as an appetizer, snack or hors d' oeuvre.

Associations

see: **appetizer, croûte, hors d'oeuvre**

Rissole

Pronounced RISOL (with i as in fit and o as in go)

potato,onion and minced beef rissoles

Origin

Rissole derives from the French **rissoler** meaning *to brown in a frying pan.* It originated with the Latin **russeolus** meaning *reddish* or *russet.* The French word **rissole** came to mean a fishball or fishcake, which was made russet brown with breadcrumbs and then browned in a frying pan.

Meaning

A **rissole** is a ball, patty or sausage-shape of finely shredded fish or meat which is tossed in beaten eggs and then covered in bread crumbs. It is sometimes necessary to refrigerate the mixture to get it to a consistency which can be readily shaped. The rissoles are fried in butter or fat until they are golden brown and crisp. They are drained and then garnished, often with parsley or chopped mushrooms.

In French cuisine, **rissoles** are also patties of puffed pastry filled with forcemeats and fried in hot oil. They are often served as appetizers or hors d'oeuvres.

Associations

Vadai are Indian rissoles made from lentils and beans. A **crépinette** is a pork rissole.

see: **appetizer, felafel, feuilletage, garnish, hors d' oeuvre**

Rissoto

Pronounced   REE-ZO-TO (with ee as in see, and o's as in go)

Origin

Riso is Italian for rice and **risotto** is Italian for *a rice dish.*

Meaning

A **risotto** is a dish made with rice (preferably Italian arborio rice which will absorb much liquid), a stock (often chicken), onions sautéed in butter, white wine or water and seasoning. There are numerous forms of risotto, depending upon what is added to the basic ingredients (e.g. simply cheese or shellfish, such as scampi). **Risotto Milanese** (which is the traditional accompaniment to **osso buco**) has bonemarrow and mushrooms added to the rice; **Risotto Napolitane** has tomatoes added. The

dish is invariably topped with the addition of grated cheese.

Associations
see: **crustacea, osso buco, paupiette, pilaf, rice**

Rollmop

Pronounced ROL-MOP (with first o as in go and second o as in got)

Origin
Roll is from the Old French **roler** meaning *to roll* or *turn like a wheel*. **Mop** derives from an Old Dutch word meaning *herring*.

Meaning
A **rollmop** is a *rolled and pickled herring fillet*. It is pickled in a

highly-seasoned marinade of vinegar or white wine or brine. It usually has shredded onions or gherkins within the roll of fish, which is held together by a small, wooden skewer or a tooth pick. It is a very popular snack or hors d'oeuvre in many European countries, especially Germany and Holland. When rollmops are sold in shops, they are usully packed in brine.

Associations
An **inglagd sil** is a Swedish *pickled herring.*
see: appetizer, fillet, hors d'oeuvre, marinade

Roulade

Pronounced
ROO-LAD (with oo as in soon and a as in rabbit)

Origin
Roulade is French for *roll*, as in roll down the hill or roll on the ground . It came to mean a dish in a tubular shape, such as a swiss-roll or a beef olive.

beef roulade

Meaning
A **roulade** is a kind of soufflé which is baked in a swiss- roll tin

(a jelly roll pan in the U.S.A.) and which is rolled around a sweet or savoury filling. In Germany, a **rouladen** is a piece of rolled beef or it is a spinach roll filled with mushrooms.

Associations

In France, a **roulé** is a gâteau in the shape of a roll, rather like a swiss-roll. A **rondelle** in French cuisine is any round disc or round slice of a food, such as a gherkin. **Braculine** in Italian means a roll of stuffed pork.

see: **paupiette**

Roux

Pronounced ROO (with oo as in soon)

Origin
Roux (or rousse) is French for *red, reddish brown* or *russet.*

Meaning
Roux (**beurre roux** in French cuisine) is made from melted butter and flour, which is slowly and carefully heated in a pan until it browns and thickens. The proportion of each ingredient is determined by the consistency or roux needed, thin or thick. Usually the proportions are equal or with slightly less flour than butter. There are three kinds of roux: white, blond and brown. The longer the cooking time, the darker the roux becomes. A roux is frequently added as a thickener to sauces (such as brown sauce, béchamel and velouté) and to stews.

Associations
A mixture (such as a roux) for thickening and binding sauces, soups and gravies is called a **liaison**. In French cuisine, a **sauce rousse** is a *brown sauce.*

see: **béchamel, ragoût, velouté**

Salad

Pronounced SAL-AD (with first a as in cat and second as in ago)

Caesar salad

Origin

Salad comes from the French **salade** and the Old Italian **salata** which derive from the Latin **sal** meaning *salt.* Salad originally meant the seasoning which accompanied a dish of herbs or raw vegetables. **Lettuce**, an important ingredient in many salads, was eaten by the kings of Persia (now Iran) in the 6th century and was a cultivated vegetable in China in the 5th century.

Meaning

A plain, simple **salad** consists of cold, crisp, fresh, well-drained, raw vegetables, which should include lettuce (**cabbage, iceberg, cos** or **Romaine**), or cole slaw. It usually includes some herbs and a dressing to moisten the vegetables. There are many dressings available, the simplest being one made from oil and vinegar. Mayonnaise is a very common salad dressing. Salads may, however, be a more substantial course and include cooked vegetables, hard-boiled eggs, cereals (e.g. rice or macaroni), meat, seafood or fish, which are invariably served cold. Some salads consist of only one vegetable which may be cooked and then served cold, as in **potato salad**, or of a variety of mixed, diced cooked vegetables, as in **Russian salad** (called **salad Olivier** in Russia). Some famous international salads are: **Waldorf salad** comprising apples, celery, walnuts, lettuce and mayonnaise; **Caesar salad** comprising cos lettuce, golden, fried-bread cubes, anchovy fillets, hard-boiled eggs, parmesan cheese and a dressing. **Fruit salads** (such as a **macédoine**) , which are usually served as a dessert, consist of fresh fruit or fruit which has been marinated in a sugar or liqueur syrup. Some salads combine vegetables and fruit, as in the famous Mexican Christmas salad, called **Ensalada de Noche Buena**, which combines a sweet dressing and a melange of fruit with cubes of beetroot and pomegranate seeds to heighten the coloured effect of the dish.

Provincial salad

Associations

A **gado gado** is an Indonesian vegetable salad which uses cooked and raw vegetables (e.g. bean sprouts, green beans, lettuce, cabbage, carrots julienne, cucumber, radishes, etc.). It is usually served with hot-chilli peanut sauce made from peanuts or peanut butter, garlic, shallots, brown sugar, water, creamed coconut, lemon juice and chilli powder. It is often accompanied by a garnish of chopped hard-boiled (hard-cooked in U.S.A.) eggs, fried onions and potatoes or chopped spring onions and prawn or shrimp crackers (called **krupuk**).

In France, salad is served as a separate course as a *re-fresher,* whereas it usually accompanies another dish in many European countries. In Spain, salad is often served before the main dish as a *pre-fresher.*

See: **cole slaw, compote, dessert, dressing, kedgeree, macédoine, mayonnaise, salami**

Salami

Pronounced
SAL-AMI (with first a as in cat, second as in father and i as in pin)

Origin
Salami (singular **salame**) derives from the Latin **sal** meaning *salt* and the Old Italian word **salame** meaning *salt meat.* Salami were first produced in Bologna in Northern Italy hundreds of years ago.

Meaning
Salami are uncooked, smoked, air-dried and fermented, seasoned sausages. They are salty and often strongly flavoured with garlic. Nowadays, they are sold in many types and sizes and are produced all over Italy and, as they preserve and travel well, are exported throughout the world. Almost all countries now have their own versions of salami. The sausage is used in antipasto, hors d'oeuvres, salads and as appetizers.

Associations
Cacciatori are small pork or beef salami made with milk in Italy
See: **antipasto, chorizo, hors d'oeuvre, salad, sausage, wurst**

Salmis

Pronounced
SAL-MEE (with a as in cat and ee as in see)

Origin
The French word **salmis** derives from the Latin **sal** meaning *salt* and the Old Italian **salame** meaning a *salt meat.* Its derivation is the same as for **salami.** Salmis is recorded as being served in France at the beginning of the 14th century. At that time meat was highly salted, in order to try to preserve it.

Meaning
Salmis is a dish (a stew, ragoût or hash) of a game bird (such

as wild duck, woodcock, pheasant, guinea fowl, partridge or pigeon), which is part roasted in an oven or on a spit for about two thirds of the full time needed. Skinned and trimmed joints of the bird are then casseroled in a separate sauce made from a stock of the carcase of the bird, wine, butter and seasoning. Sometimes onions, tomatoes, mushrooms, potatoes, thyme and lemon juice are added. The dish is often served on a large croûton with accompanying vegetables.

Associations
See: **casserole, croûte, ragoût**

Saltimboca

Pronounced SAL-TEEM-BOKA (with first a as in salt,, ee as in see and o as in go and final a as in far)

Origin
In Italian **salt** means *jump,* **im** means *into* and **boca** means *mouth,* so **saltimboca** literally means *jump into the mouth,* implying that the dish is very tasty. The dish originated in Rome.

Meaning
Saltimboca consists of thin slices of ham (proscuttio) laid on fillets of veal,which have been seasoned with sage and sautéed in butter. They are then braised in white wine. The dish is served with pasta , vegetables or salad.

Associations
See: **fillet, prosciutto , vitello tonnato**

Sambal

Pronounced SAM-BAL (with first a as in lamb and second as in far)

Origin
Sambal is of Malaysian and Indonesian origin. It means a

highly-seasoned condiment.

Meaning

A **sambal** (also spelled **sambaal** and **sambel**) is a condiment made from raw vegetables and fruit with spices and vinegar. It usually contains chillies. There are various kinds of sambals. **Sambal bajak** has fried spices; **sambal terasi** includes shrimp paste; **sambal ulek** consists of red chillies which have been crushed with salt in a mortar. Sambals accompany most Malaysian and Indonesian dishes.

Associations

see: satay

Sashimi

Pronounced SASHEEMI (with a as in pan, ee as in see and i **as in pin)**

Origin
Sashimi is Japanese for *raw fish in slices.* Literally the word means *pierced flesh.* The dish in its present form has been served since the 17th century, when soya sauce became popular.

Meaning
Sashimi consists of the freshest, top-quality, raw fish. In Japan for instance, it might be fillets of tuna, bonito, salmon, halibut, sea bream or mackerel, whichever is in season. It is sliced into bite-size portions and dressed into different shapes. The Japanese appreciate the texture and translucent qualities of fresh, raw fish. Usually, it is served with pickles, vinegar, soya sauce, **wasabi** (which is a green horse-radish paste which is often mixed with soya sauce), or with **daikon**, which is a very large, white radish. In Japanese cuisine, much care is taken to ensure that the fish is presented with its garnishes in the most aesthetically-pleasing way.

Associations
Gravalax is a Swedish speciality of raw salmon which is cured with sugar and seasoning. It is served with mustard sauce. **Kokoda** is a Fijian dish and **seviche** or **ceviche** is a Mexican and South American dish, both of which consist of raw fish which are marinated in lemon and lime juices.
See: dressing, marinade, soya

Satay

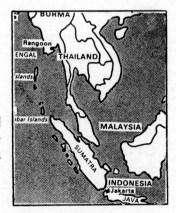

Pronounced   SAT-AY (with a as in bat and ay as in say)

Origin
In Malaysia the word **satay** is used and in Indonesia **sate** is used to describe the same dish, where food is served on a skewer.

Meaning
A **satay** is made by cutting up bite-sized pieces of meat, fish or poultry, which are then pushed onto a bamboo skewer about 10

cms long. The satay is then grilled over a fire, traditionally using charcoal. They are like miniature **shish kebabs**. Traditionally, the satays are served in Indonesia and Malaya with a peanut sauce, made from peanut butter, sugar, lemon juice and **sambal oelek**, which is finely-minced red chillies mixed with salt and soya sauce.

Associations
See: **brochette, chilli, kebab, sambal, soya**

Sauerbrauten

Pronounced SOWA-BROWTEN (with ow's as in cow, a as in ago and e as in lemon)

Origin
Sauer is German for *sour* and **brauten** for *a roast*. Literally, it means a *sour roast* (of meat), as originally the meat was marinated in vinegar. The meat is not sour but it has a distinctive flavour. It has been one of the most popular dishes

in Germany for hundreds of years and it varies from region to region.

Meaning

The German *pot roast* **sauerbrauten** is made by marinating beef for up to four days in a marinade, which, traditionally, can be buttermilk in North Germany, beer in South Germany (Bavaria) and white wine, vinegar, carrots and onions in Central Germany. The meat is then browned and simmered in a marinade of sliced onions, bay leaf and cloves until very tender. It is often served with potato pancakes and vegetables.

Associations

See: **marinade, pomme, sweet and sour**

Sauerkraut

Pronounced SOWA -KROWT (with ow's as in cow and a as in ago)

Origin
Sauerkraut derives from the Old German **sür** meaning *sour* and **krüt** meaning *cabagge*. The name originated in Austria. The technique of making sauerkraut is recorded in Ancient Roman documents and it is almost certain that the Romans learned the process from the Orient. It formed part of the diet of workers who were constructing the Great Wall of China. Pickled cabbage was introduced into Britain by the Romans. It was introduced into Austria in the 13th century and then into Germany and Alsace Lorraine in Eastern France and it became a very popular dish in all three countries.

Meaning
Sauerkraut is made by placing alternate layers of shredded, drumhead cabbage and salt in a closed container, such as a wooden barrel or a very large stone jar, the top of which is covered with muslin. The cabbage is fermented with juniper berries for about four weeks. It is served as a garnish to meat and wurst dishes but it is also used in combination with other foods.

Associations
Sauerkraut is called **choucroute** (**chou** is French for *cabbage* and **croute** for *crust*). in France. It is often referred to as **pickled cabbage** in many English speaking countries. In Italy, it is called **craut**. It is available in tins in some delicatessens. In Germany, a pie called **sauerkrautkuchen**, which has sauerkraut as a main ingredient, is popular.
A dish which is served in Germany with sauerkraut is **eisbein**. **Eis** is German for *ice* or *cold* and **bein** for *leg*. An **eisbein** is the top part of the front leg of a pig or the pig's knuckle. The pork is boiled and then refrigerated to keep it cold. **Kasseler rippen** consists of smoked, cured ribs of pork on a bed of sauerkraut, accompanied by mashed potatoes. The meat may also be served with red cabbage and potato dumplings. A rich sauce made from red wine and sour cream is often served with the dish. A very popular dish in Korea is **Kimchi**, which is cabbage pickled in garlic and chillis.
See: **garnish, goulash, wurst**

Sausage

Pronounced SOS-IJ (with o as in got and i as in pin)

Origin

Sausage derives from the Latin **salsus** meaning *salted*. **Sauce** has the same derivation. There is evidence to show that the Chinese were using salt to preserve meat in the 13th century B.C. The Ancient Greeks and Romans also preserved meats with salt. In Old French, a highly-salted minced meat which was stuffed into the inside of an ox or some other meat was called **saussiche**. The salt was used not only to flavour meat but also to preserve it. In France today, a **saucisse** is a small sausage which is eaten hot and a **saucisson** is a dried, preserved, large sausage that does not need cooking and is eaten cold. Sausages have been eaten throughout the world for hundreds of years and before refrigeration was invented the hotter countries tended to have saltier sausages than the cooler countries, as there was a greater need for preserving the meat. The earliest written reference to sausage is in the *Odyssey*, written in the 9th century B.C. by the Ancient Greek poet, Homer. From the Middle Ages, sausages have taken their names from their places of origin, such as the Bologna sausage from Bologna in Italy, the Frankfurter from Frankfurt in Germany.

Meaning
There is a huge selection of sausages available today, which are made in a variety of ways (e.g. fresh, dried, seasoned, smoked etc.) to give distinctive flavours. Most sausages are made from minced beef or pork, or mixtures of both, with herbs and spices added, which are enclosed in a caul (the thin, lacy membrane which encloses the stomach of an animal) or in an animal's intestines. Some are ready to eat without cooking (known as **dry sausage**); some need to be cooked (known as **wet sausage**). Each country has sausages which are a speciality - for example, **bratwurst** and **franfurters** from Germany, **mortadella**, **zampone**, **Bologna** and **peperone** from Italy, **chorizo** from Spain and Mexico, **saveloy** and **sausisson de Toulouse** from France, **rookwurst** from Holland, **kabanos** from Poland, **merguez** from Tunisia, **coppa** from Corsica, **black pudding** from England. **Choong** are Chinese smoked sausages made from pork or chicken livers. The Japanese have a fish sausage called **kamaboko**, which is sold in tins.

Associations
A **chipolata** is a small Italian sausage made from pork, fat, seasoning and a little brandy, or a dish which contains Italian sausages. It can also refer to a mincemeat with which sausages are served. A **chorizo** is a Spanish and Mexican sausage made from smoked pork or a mixture of pork and beef. It is usually a bright red colour. It is flavoured with pimiento (hot red pepper) and is strong and hot. It is served fried or raw (*cru*) and is a popular breakfast food in Mexico. It is often served with mashed chickpeas in Spain. **Erwten soep** is a Dutch pea and sausage soup.
See: **charcuterie, chorizo, croûte, frankfurter, mortadella, paella, salami, wurst**

Savarin

Pronounced
SAVA-RAN (with a's as in cat and an as in a naselised an in sang)

Origin
In the mid 1850's, a French pastry cook changed a **baba's** shape, left out the raisins in the dish and renamed the cake after Jean

Brillat-Savarin, a famous gastronome who produced books on cuisine. The new cake was called a **savarin**.

Meaning

Savarin dough is made from sifted, plain flour, dried yeast, sugar, salt, beaten eggs and soft butter or milk. In French cuisine, it is called **pâte à . savarin**. A buttered ring mould, called a **savarin mould**, which has a sunken centre and a raised border, is used. When the dough is cooked, the cake is soaked in a liqueur-flavoured syrup, made from honey, water and a liqueur or spirit, which is traditionally rum or kirsch (a German cherry-brandy). The centre of the savarin may be filled with chantilly cream (and called a **savarin chantilly**) or glazed cherries (and called a **savarin montmorency**) to make a delicious and luxurious dessert.

Associations

Pasta frolla is a delicate Italian sweet pastry which is similar to a savarin pastry.
See: baba, crème, kugelhopf, gâteau, pâte

Scallopini

Pronounced SKA-LO-PEENEE (with a as in far, o as in got, and ee's as in see)

Origin

Scallopine derives from the Swedish **kalops** (and in dialect **kollops**) meaning *slices of beef which are stewed* . The word derived from this in English is **collop**, which is used in the Bible and has a very long ancestry.

Meaning

A **scallopine** (plural **scallopini**) is an Italian dish which uses thin slices of veal. Well-known and popular dishes are **scallopine alla panna** (veal fillet with cream), **scallopine al marsala** (veal fillet with a sauce made with marsala wine) **scallopine di vitello ripiene** (veal fillet made into a sandwich and stuffed (*repiene*) with mushroom and ham fillings and topped with mozzarella cheese).

Associations

Escallop (also spelled **escalope**) means a thin, round and flattened, boneless slice of meat or fish but the term is usually applied to a slice of veal or a pork fillet. An **escallop** is usually coated with a seasoned flour then dipped in beaten egg and coated with bread crumbs. It is then fried in butter and oil. The word can also refer to meat, fish or poultry which is served in a **scallop shell**.
See: **cordon bleu, schnitzel, vitello tonato**

Schnitzel

Pronounced SHNIT-ZUL (with i as in bit and u as in uncle)

Origin
Schnitzel is German for a *slice.* The **schnitzel**, as a dish, originated in Milan in the 19th century, although breaded veal chops had been cooked in Italy for many years before this. The dish was taken to Vienna in Austria and had universal fame as the **Wienner** (*Viennese*) **schnitzel.**

Meaning
A **schnitzel** is a cutlet (escalope) of veal which is beaten out between grease-proof paper until it is about 30 mm thick. Lemon juice is then squeezed over the cutlet, which is left to marinate in the juice for about an hour. The marinating helps to tenderise the meat. **Plain schnitzels** (or **schnitzels naturel**) are then fried in butter or oil. To make **Wienner schnitzels**, however,the cutlets are coated with bread crumbs or seasoned flour and fried in butter until they are golden brown. The dish is garnished with wedges of lemon and served with vegetables or salad.

Associations
The word schnitzel usually refers to veal dishes but it can be used for other meat, such as **turkey schnitzels. Tonkatsu**, which is made from fried pork, is the Japanese equivalent of the **Wienner schnitzel.**
See: **crème, cordon bleu, scallopini, vitello tonato**

Scone

Pronounced   SKON (with o either as in gone or stone)

Origin
Scone is a shortened version of the Dutch **schoonbrot** or German **schönbrot** meaning *beautiful bread* or *fine bread*. It was a round cake made from fine wheatmeal flour which was baked on a griddle. Scones were made by early settlers in countries like the United Sates as a substitute for bread. They were quickly and easily made.

Meaning
Scones (called biscuits in the U.S.A.) are made (a number is usually called a **batch**) from a dough of fresh self-raising flour, butter, salt and milk (or milk and water to make very light scones). They can be made sweet by the addition of sugar or honey and by the inclusion of sultanas or dates. They can be cooked on the top of stews or casseroles to form a crust or as dumplings. The dough can also be used as a base for a pizza. They can be served hot or cold and are popular with jam and cream or with cheese as a snack.

Associations
See: **casserole, dumpling, pizza**

Seaweed

Pronounced   SEE-WEED (with ee's as in see)

Origin
Seaweed or **sea wrack** (from wreck that is cast ashore), as it is sometimes called, has been used as food for hundreds of years by people in Northern Europe, especially in times of food scarcity. In Japan it has been eaten for thousands of years and continues to be a very popular food in various forms, or is used in combination with other foods as a condiment.

Meaning
Carragheen (also called **Irish** or **Iberian moss**) is a seaweed which is used in Ireland to thicken soups and sauces. In Wales, **lavabread** is made from **lava** which is rolled in oatmeal and served with bacon. **Dulse** is eaten raw in salads in New England (U.S.A.) and is also used in a relish. **Lava**, one type called **nori** and another **wakame**, is cultivated in Japan and is sold as dried, thin, black sheets. It is used as a garnish to many dishes and is lightly toasted and crumpled onto salad. It is put into soups, pickles and preserves and is used as wrapper for rice in **sushi**. **Kombu** (dried **kelp**) is essential in Japan in the flavouring of **dashi**, one of its principal sauces, and is also used in dips and in relishes. **Hijiki** is a seaweed which is used as a vegetable in Japan. **Agar agar**, which is obtained from seaweed, is an effective setting-agent for making sweets and desserts.

Associations
See: **dashi, garnish, miso, rice, salad, sushi**

Semolina

Pronounced   SEMA -LEENA (with e as in get, a's as in ago and ee as in see)

Origin
Semolina is from the Latin **semila** meaning *wheat meal* and the Italian **semolino**, which is a smaller version of **semola** meaning the hard grain left over after the sifting of flour.

Meaning

Semolina is the coarsest grade of milled wheat. It is made from the middling (endosperm) of **durum**, the hardest kind of wheat grown. It is sieved to obtain three grades: coarse, medium and fine, but it is never as fine as flour. It is used in the making of very stiff doughs for spaghetti, macaroni and other shaped pastas. It is also used to make **semolina pudding**, which is made in a bain marie with eggs and cream. The semolina which is bought for puddings is called **farina** in the U.S.A. and **Breakfast Delight** in Australia.

Associations

Halva is a sweet dish eaten in Greece, Turkey and Middle East countries. It is made from semolina, oil, flavoured sugar, chopped almonds, cinnamon, fruit, chocolate, spices and flower petals. **Irmir helvasi** is an almond and semolina custard which is a very popular dessert in Turkey. Semolina is enjoyed in India, where it is called **sooji**.
See: **almond, bain marie, couscous, croquette, gnocchi, pasta, polenta**

Smörgåsbord

Pronounced SMORGAS- BORD
(with or's as in port, a as in cat)

Origin

Smörgås is Swedish for *bread-and-butter* and **bord** for *table*. A tradition was begun in Sweden at the end of the 1880's, especially in country areas, where each family brought to a party in one house its own hot or cold speciality dish. The larger the party, the more

different dishes there were. All the contributions were placed on the smörgåsbord.

Meaning

For a **smörgåsbord**, dishes are laid out on a large, long table. Guests help themselves to the dishes which attract them, although traditionally fish is taken first, meat (including meatballs) and salads next and desserts and cheese last. A variety of breads (including Swedish knäckbröd and lefse) and open sandwiches are important parts of the assortment, as are a variety of condiments. Many restaurants now offer a smörgåsbord of a large variety of hot and cold dishes, especially for brunch or luncheon. A fixed price is paid by patrons, who may help themselve from one table or from a number of tables.

Associations

A popular, traditional dish served on smörgåsbords in Sweden is **Jansson's temptation**, consisting of potatoes, onions and anchovies which are baked in cream. The Danish version of a smörgåsbord is called a **smørrebrad** which has a vast assortment of open sandwiches. The Finnish version is called a **voilei päpöytä**. An Indonesian version is the **rijsttafel** (see **rice**). A **buffet** is a meal where guests help themselves to a variety of hot and cold, sweet and savoury dishes placed on a long table or a number of tables.

Sorbet

Pronounced SO-BAY (with o as in port and ay as in say)

Origin

Sorbet derives from the Arabic *shariba* meaning *he drank*. A **sharab** was an Arabic beverage. **Sorbets** (also called **sherbets**) were introduced (along with ice cream) to Europeans by Arabs, who themselves had learned how to make them from the Chinese. Originally, European sorbets were made from liqueurs, heavy wines or fruit juices.

Meaning

A **sorbet** is a light, frozen mixture of diluted, puréed fruit, fruit juices, caster sugar and water (or a sugar syrup) and egg white. Sometimes it is enriched with Italian meringue mixture. It is frozen and

raspberry sorbet

served straight from a refigerator or freezer in goblets or coupes. During a meal of a number of courses, it may be served as a palate cleanser and refresher. Nowadays, vegetable sorbets (e.g tomato sorbet) are also served.

Associations
See: meringue, purée

Soubise

Pronounced SOO-BEES (with oo as in moon and ee as in see)

Origin
Soubise is named after Charles de Rohan, Prince of Soubise, a commander of the French armies in the 18th century.

Meaning
A **soubise sauce** is a variant of **béchamel sauce**, which is added to a purée of onions and cream. A **soubise** is also a purée of onions or onions and rice to which is added nutmeg and seasoning. It is served with eggs, mutton or veal. The term **soubise** in French cuisine (as in **à la soubise**) implies that onions, or an onion purée, are a main ingredient in a dish.

Associations
See: béchamel, à la (Lyonnaise), purée

Soufflé

Pronounced SOO-FLAY (with oo as in soon and ay as in say)

Origin
Soufflé is derived from the French **souffler** meaning *to blow,* which originated from the Latin **sufflare** meaning *to blow under.* In contemporary French, **soufflé** means *blown, breathed* or *whispered.* The word suggests the fragility and lightness of the dish called a **soufflé**, which has been made in France since the 18th century. The soufflé is one of the 500 egg recipes which

are attributed to French haute cuisine.

Meaning
A **soufflé** is a very light, foamy concoction made from egg whites which are folded into a sauce of egg yolks, milk and, sometimes, flour. **Savoury soufflés** may include in their mixture grated cheese, meat, shellfish, fish or fish purées or vegetables, such as spinach. **Sweet soufflés** include sugar and fruit purées, chocolate or liqueurs. The mixture is baked at a moderate heat to produce a dish which is uniformly cooked. A soufflé can be served as a main course with meat or fish or as an appetizer. It should be served as soon as it is made to avoid the collapse of such an airy creation. The term also refers to a very lightly- baked or fluffy steamed pudding.

Associations
A **soufflé** in Italian is a **sformato**.
See: **appetizer, charlotte, crème, meringue, omelette, purée**

Soya

Pronounced   SOY-A (with oy as in boy and a as in ago)

Origin

The word **soya** derives from the Chinese **shi-yu** meaning *salted bean*. The soya bean plant originated in China and its cultivation spread to Japan and Korea. Recorded evidence shows that it was one of the most important crops in China in 2800 B.C. For thousands of years it has been known in the Far East as "the meat of the earth", as it is one of the few sources of complete protein. It was brought to Europe in 1712 by a German botanist named Engelbert Kalmfer but it was not until the 20th century that it was cultivated as a food on a large scale. Today China and the United States are the principal cultivators of soya. The plant's tender green pods can be eaten as a vegetable and its seeds are a legume, which are used in a wide range of sauces, relishes and dips. Brewed **soya sauce** was produced in the Orient more than 2500 years ago. The Kikkoman Corporation, the largest producer of soya sauce in Japan and in the world, was making soya sauce commercially in 1630.

Meaning

The **soya bean** or **soy bean** (also called **haba soya** or **preta**) is used extensively in Asian, Chinese and Japanese cuisine. **Soya sauce** can be light or dark. The light is usually used with fish, seafood and soup dishes, the dark with meat dishes. **Beancurd,** which is made from soya beans, is a staple food of Japan and China. In Japan it is called **tofu,** in China **dow foo pok. Oyster sauce**, which is popular in Chinese cuisine is made from oysters cooked in soya sauce and brine. **Hot black bean sauce** (also called **chilli bean sauce**) is made from soya beans and ground, hot chillies. **Hoisin sauce,** which is used as a dip and in barbecued pork dishes, is made from soya beans, garlic and spices. All three sauces are very popular in Chinese cuisine, as is **miso**, which is made from soya beans and salt, in Japanese cuisine.

Associations

In Japan, soya sauce is called **shoyu**, in Indonesia **ketjay**, in France **piquante sauce de soya**, in Germany **sosse von soja**, in Italy **salsa di soia**.
See: miso, sashimi, spring rolls, sukiyaki, tempura, teriyaki, tofu

Spaghetti

Pronounced SPA-GETEE (with a as in cat, e as in get and ee as in see)

Origin

In Italian, **spago** means *cord, thread* or *string*. **Spaghetti** means *little cords* or *strings.* Spaghetti is the plural of spaghetto. Spaghetti, in the form of long strings of pasta, originated in the South of Italy in the Naples area.

Meaning

Spaghetti is made from durum wheat in the shape of long strings of pasta. It is not tubular, as is macaroni. It is finer than macaroni and coarser than vermicelli. It is one of the most popular forms of pasta in Italy and, indeed, the world. It should be cooked in enough water for it to absorb water and still leave sufficient water for cooking. It usually takes about 12 minutes to cook *al dente.* A popular accompaniment to spaghetti is **bolognese sauce**, which is sprinkled with parmesan cheese.

Associations

See: al dente, bolognese, macaroni, parmigiano, pasta

spaghetti with basil

Spanikopita

Pronounced
SPANI-KOPITA (with a's as in cat, i's as in pin, o as in got)

Origin
Spanikopita is Greek for *spinach,* a plant which originated in Persia (now Iran) thousands of years ago. Traders took the plant into Europe and it became a popular vegetable in England in the 1500's.

Meaning
Spanikopita consists of a mixture of feta cheese and shredded cooked spinach. Sometimes eggs are added. Feta cheese is a crumbly white Greek cheese which is made from goat's milk. It is often salty, unless it is soaked in milk. The cheese-spinach mixture is baked in filo pastry. The pastries are served hot as appetizers or snacks.

Associations
See: appetizer, filo

Spring rolls

Pronounced
SPRING -ROLS (with i as in sing and o as in go)

Origin
Spring rolls come from the **Fukien** school of Chinese cuisine. There are five schools, namely **Canton, Fukien, Szechuen, Shanghai** and **Peking.** As most of the restaurants outside China are managed by Cantonese Chinese, Cantonese cuisine has become better known throughout the world than the others. The word Spring was used in English to describe the rolls as fresh Spring vegetables were used as a filling. In China, they are called **popiah.**

Meaning
Spring rolls consist of thin barrel-shaped pastry packages which are stuffed with savoury fillings and deep fried. They resemble rolled pancakes. The wrappers are made from very thin sheets of pastry made from rice flour , salt , beaten eggs and

water. As the pastry sheets are difficult to make, they are usually bought from shops. The range of fillings is very wide and can be of vegetables, minced meat, shredded fish or shellfish. The filling is usually mixed with soya sauce, ginger, oil, rice wine, seasoning and spices. Trays of a variety of spring rolls are offered in Chinese restaurants as appetizers.

Associations

A number of countries have savoury-filled, deep-fried spring rolls in their diet, made with rice paper wrappers. In Vietnam , spring rolls are called **cha gio,** in Japan **haru maki** and in Asia **poppia se.**
See: **appetizers, crêpe, rice, soya**

Stock

Pronounced STOK (with o as in got)

Origin

Stock derives from the Old English **stocc** meaning *a stick, a stump, post* or *handle.* It came to mean something which supports or acts as a foundation. It was then used in cuisine to mean any liquid that formed the basis for a soup or sauce.

Meaning

It is recognised among chefs that a good **stock** is essential in the preparation of savoury food. The French call stocks **les fonds de cuisine** meaning *the foundations of cooking.* Stocks are made from various kinds of meat, poultry, seafood or fish and vegetables, with herbs and spices. There are meat stocks, chicken stocks, white stocks (using white meat - such as veal), vegetable stocks and double stocks or consommé. The combined ingredients must be simmered slowly, often for hours, and strained until all the flavours have been concentrated and the essence of the ingredients has been extracted. Stocks are used in making sauces, soups, stews and casseroles and for thickening. They can be easily frozen, so that they can be readily available immediately when required. Potatoes and parsnips are not used in stocks as they cloud them. Cabbage is avoided as it tends to give a stock a sour flavour and fat should be not be used and removed from meat.

Associations

Fumet (which is French for *smell*, especially the pleasant smell of food cooking) is made by boiling meat or fish with or without vegetables in stock or wine until a highly-concentrated, well-flavoured liquid is obtained. It is added to stocks or sauces to give them body. It is most often used for poaching fish or as an addition to a fish sauce. The reduction (thickening) of a meat stock to a strong, thick consistency makes it into a **demi glace**, which is a brown, Espagnole sauce. In French cuisine , a white stock, based on chicken or veal, is called a **blanc**; a brown meat stock is called an **estouffade**. The Italian for stock is **battuto**. It usually consists of finely-chopped vegetables, herbs and salt pork or oil. **Brühe** or **suppenstock** is German for a stock. **Dashi** is used as a stock in Japan.

See: casserole, consommé, dashi, mulligatawny, panada, paupiette, pilaf, velouté

Stollen

Pronounced STOL- AN (with o as in got and a as in ago)

Christmas stollen

Origin
Stollen (or **stolle**) is German for *a fruit loaf.*

221

Meaning

A **stollen** is a German loaf-shaped cake made with yeast dough, chopped almonds, chopped dried fruit (currants, candied orange peel, lemon peel, lemon rind etc.), a few drops of vanilla essence, a little rum, a large cup of warm milk and some bitter almonds. The baked loaf is sprinkled liberally with fine sugar. It is usually eaten on festive occasions in Germany.

Associations

A cake similar to the stollen is the Polish **strutzel**.
See: almond, gâteau

Strudel

Pronounced STROO-DAL (with oo as in soon and a as in ago)

Origin

Strudel derives from the Old German **streden** meaning *to bubble* or *boil* and **stridel** meaning an *eddy* or *whirlpool*. The word was probably used to describe the pastry called strudel because the flakes of pastry after baking crinkle and wrinkle and appear to bubble. The strudel originated in Bavaria in the south of Germany and in Austria.

Meaning
A **strudel** is a dessert with a delicate casing made of paper-thin layers of filo pastry, each of which is brushed with butter. The Austrians say the pastry is so thin that you can read a love letter through it! The casing usually has a filling of cooked, diced fruit, chopped almonds, a little cinnamon and sometimes a little brandy. Some strudels include soft cheese. The best-known strudel is **apple strudel** (in German **apfel strudel**) and another popular strudel is **kirschen strudel**, which has a filling of stoned cherries. When baked, the strudels are sprinkled with fine sugar and then are eaten hot or cold, as a snack or a dessert, often accompanied by fresh or whipped cream. There is also a vegetable strudel.

Associations
See: **almond, filo**

Sukiyaki

Pronounced   SOOKI -YAKEE (with oo as in soon, i as in pin, a as in sand and ee as in see)

Origin
In Japanese, **suki** means a *spade* with a hollowed out blade or **scoop** and **yaki** means *to grill* or *broil*. During the 16th century in Japan, Buddhist monks forbade villagers, who were Buddhists, to eat the meat of four-footed animals, such as cattle or horses. Some villagers, to avoid being seen by the monks and some of their fellow villagers who kept to the rules and also to avoid tainting their household cooking utensils with the forbidden meat, went into the fields near where they lived and cooked meat by grilling it over an open fire, using their spades to hold the meat over the hot fire. They called the meat **sukiyaki**. The dish has been popular in Japan since about 1864.

Meaning
Sukiyaki is a dish made from slices of prime rump or sirloin

steak which are cooked in a little hot oil for about 3 to 5 minutes. The meat is basted with a **sukiyaki sauce** made from sugar, sake, mirin and soya sauce. Tofu (beancurd), mushrooms, chopped leeks and spinach and **shirataki**, translucent, jelly-like noodles, are then put in the pot. It is one of the dishes which the Japanese call a **nabemono**, meaning *one-pot table-cooking*. Ingredients are cooked in a common pot and all help themselves from the pot, usually while the food continues to cook at the table. The procedure is similar to that when a group of people is eating bagna cauda in Italy or fondue in Switzerland. In Japan, each person has an individual side dish of raw egg and morsels from the pot may be dipped in the egg before being eaten. Sukiyaki is one of the most popular dishes in Japan.

Associations
See: **bagna cauda, fillet, fondue, mirin, noodles, soya, tofu**

Sundae

Pronounced SUN-DAY (u as in fun and ay as in say)

Origin
Sundae originated in the United States. It probably derives from the word **Sunday**, a time when some people, particularly teenagers, would visit a store to eat icecream. The owner of the stores concocted a dish from the left-over ice creams from the previous week and they called the concoction a sundae. The *word* sundae was probably used to avoid using the word Sunday for a dessert, which would have offended some people.

Meaning
A **sundae** consists of a number of different flavoured ice creams (e.g. vanilla, strawberry, banana, chocolate sauce) mixed with fresh or crystallised fruit, chopped nuts and sometimes fresh or chantilly cream. It is usually served in a tall glass (e.g. a champagne glass) or a silver cup. Often it is topped with fruit, such as raspberries and maraschino cherries, and a sprig of mint.

Associations

Sundaes are called **coupes,** meaning *ice cups,* in France. Coupe is used in many cookery books, for example **cherry coupe, peach coupe** and **apricot coupe.**

Sûpreme

Pronounced SOO-PREEM (with oo as in soon and ee as in see)

Origin

Sûpreme is French for *the best* or *the highest* in achievement.

Meaning

Sûpreme describes a special manner of cooking and presenting dishes in **haute cuisine,** which denotes that only the finest ingredients have been used. **Chicken sûpreme** (*sûpreme de volaille*) is the *breast of chicken.* **Sauce sûpreme** is made from velouté sauce enriched with cream, which is served with chicken breasts or egg or vegetable dishes. The term **sûpreme** is also

chicken sûpreme

used in French cuisine to describe a large fillet of fish (e.g. of halibut) which is cut on the slant into portions.

Associations
See: cuisine, fillet, haute cuisine, poularde, velouté

Sushi

preparing sushi

Pronounced
SOO-SHEE (with oo as in moon and ee as in see)

Origin
Sushi is a Japanese word, which originally meant *sour* or *vinegary* and later came to mean *pickled fish*. Imperial records in Kyoto in Japan in the 10th century show that fish was salted and tnen preserved between layers of rice for periods of from one to three years. The rice fermented and became flavoured with a vinegary taste, which the Japanese discovered much to their liking. A dish called **shushi** developed, where rice was flavoured with vinegar. The rice, called **meshi**, became very popular. **Nigrizushi**, hand-made shushi, originated in the early 19th century and became not only a method of shushi preparation but a culinary art. There is now a very wide range of **nigri-zushi** in Japanese cuisine. Other sushi are **hazozushi**, where sushi are elegantly presented in boxes; **makizushi**, which is rolled sushi and **chirashizushi**, or "*scatttered sushi*" , consisting of minced vegetables with rice, topped with colourful seaweed and eggs.

Meaning
Sushi (or **osushi**, as the Japanese use an honorific **o** in formal speech, as a

Photograph kindly supplied by
Kikkoman Corporation

226

sign of respect for the person addressed), sometimes called *the Japanese sandwich,* is made from short-grained rice which is flavoured with a sweet rice vinegar. The rice is shaped into various forms·of about bite size and then topped with a savoury morsel, such as flavoured fish or seafood or vegetables. Probably the best-known **shushi** (or **otsukuri** as it is also called) is where vinegared rice and raw fish or seafood are wrapped in konbu or nori seaweed to make a shaped package. Sushi is usually served with a garnish of ginger (gari), green horseradish (wasabi) and soya sauce. It

Photograph kindly supplied by
Kikkoman Corporation

is estimated that there are now as many as ten thousand shushi shops in Tokyo alone, which shows its enormous popularity in Japan.

Associations
In Japan "bags" of **abura-age** (see **tofu**) are filled with sushi and a little rice vinegar or dashi to make a favourite snack.
See: dashi, mirin, miso, rice, tofu, seaweed (kombu

Sweet and Sour

Pronounced
SWEET and SOWA (with ee as in see , ow as in cow and a as in ago)

Origin
The combination of sweet and sour flavours has been used in cuisines throughout the world for hundreds of years. The Chinese and Japanese particularly have used the method. The Ancient Romans combined sweet and sour tastes in some of their sauces, using peppermint, sultanas, currants, carrots, honey, vinegar and oil. The sauces became known as **agrodolce sauces, agro** being Italian for *sour* and **dolce** for *sweet.*

Meaning
Meat, fish and poultry dishes are given a sweet and sour flavour

by the addition of a sauce which contains both sweet and acid and spicy tastes. A sweet and sour sauce usually consists of a stock into which is put sugar, some sweet puréed or grated fruit (pineapple is very popular) and a sweet sauce, such as plum sauce. Ginger, soya sauce and vinegar, tomato sauce and red pepper are added to provide the tangy, spicy and sour flavour. Cornflour can be added to thicken the sauce and water or wine, if the sauce needs to be diluted. The main dish of pork, chicken or fish is covered with the sweet and sour sauce and then served with garnishes.

Associations
Prawn pathia is an Indian sweet and sour dish made from coconut, tomatoes , spices and prawns.
See: sauerbrauten, yoghurt

Sweetbread

Pronounced SWEET - BRED (with ee as in see and e as in fed)

Origin
Sweet is from the Latin **suavis** meaning *pleasant* and **bread** is from the Old English **bread** which was originally a *bit* or *piece of food.* The word **sweetbread** was used for centuries to mean a *tasty, pleasant morsel of food,* but nowadays it has very precise meaning in cuisine.

Meaning
Sweetbread is the name given in cuisine to the thymus (less often the pancreas) gland of calves or lambs. The thymus gland is situated near the base of the neck at the top of the chest and the pancreas is in the belly region of the animal. The flesh of the sweetbread is soft and white. Some people consider it a delicacy. It is first blanched to ensure complete whiteness and then it is braised in a white or brown stock or grilled. It is served with a garnish of vegetables . It is sometimes included as an ingredient in a pâté.

Associations
In French cuisine, it is called **ris d' agneau.**
See: pâté, timbale, velouté, vol au vent

Tahini

Pronounced TA-EENI (with first a as in father, ee as in see and i as in pin)

Origin
Tahini is derived from **tahina** , which is the Arabic word for *to grind* or *crush*. The dish originated in the Middle East and has been eaten for thousands of years in Syria, Lebanon, Iran, Iraq, Palestine, Jordan, Saudi Arabia, Israel and Egypt.

Meaning
Tahini (also spelled **tahine**) is an oily paste made from crushed sesame seeds. It has a nutty flavour. When it is mixed with mashed chickpeas, lemon juice and garlic, it makes a dip called **hummus** (also spelled **homus**) which is very popular in cuisines from Greece to Israel. Mixed with olive oil and puréed lentils, it is eaten with pita bread as an appetizer (**mezze**) or hors d'oeuvre.

Associations
see: **appetizer, chickpeas, dahl, hors d'oeuvre, mezze, purée**

Tandoori

Pronounced TAN-DOORI (with a as in father, oo as in moon and i as in pin)

Origin
Tandoori is Punjabi (in Northern India) for *in the oven* , referring to a tandoor oven.

Meaning
A **tandoor** is a vat-shaped clay oven (rather like a large Ali Baba jar) which, in India, is usually set into the ground with its top level with the floor. This makes it very well insulated and it is able to generate intense heat. It is traditionally heated from its

base by a charcoal or wood fire. Probably the best-known **tandoori** dish is **tandoori chicken** (called **tandoori murgh**) which is chicken marinated in yoghurt and garam masala and then cooked on a skewer (called in India a **tikka**) which is lowered over the red-hot coals. The fierce heat of the oven seals the meat being cooked and the natural juices are retained so the chicken is not dry. The sides of the oven are used to bake **naan** and other bread. The dough sticks to the sides and is removed , after being quickly baked.

Associations
see: **garam masala, naan, yoghurt**

Tapenade

Pronounced   TAPA-NAD (with first a as in cat, second as in ago and third as in made)

Origin
The term **tapenade** derives from the French Provençal word **tapéno** meaning a *caper.*
Capers are the small pickled buds of a small, prickly bush (the capparis spinosa) which grows in Mediterranean countries, such as France, Italy and Spain and in the United States. The dish, **tapenade**, was invented by a chef in Marseilles in Provence in Southern France in the 19th century.

Meaning
A **tapenade** is a relish, sauce or spread consisting of pounded black olives, anchovy fillets and well-strained capers which are blended with olive oil, strong mustard, lemon juice and seasoning. It is a strongly-flavoured sauce or pâté which is served with cold fish, beef and eggs or is spread on hot toast as a snack or an hors d'oeuvre. It can be purchased in jars.

Associations
Nasturtium seeds, which have a pungent taste, are sometimes soaked in salt water and used instead of capers in a tapenade .

Taramasalata

Pronounced TARA -MASA-LATHA (with with a's as in cat)

Origin
Taramasalata is derived from the Greek **tarama** meaning *cod roe* and **salata** meaning *salad.* The word salata was used as the mixture was used as a salad dressing.

Meaning
Taramasalata is a dip made from the smoked, dried roe (eggs) of the cod or the grey mullet, which is pounded with olive oil, garlic, soaked bread, lemon juice and seasoning into a smooth paste. Sometimes a tomato purée is added to colour it and to sharpen the flavour. Also, chopped hard-boiled eggs are sometimes added. It is served with lemon juice as a dip or is spread on toast or unleavened bread, like a pâté, as an appetizer or hors d' oeuvre. As the Greeks and Turks love **dolmades**, taramasalata is used as a filling for hollowed hard-boiled eggs, tomatoes and other vegetables. They are one of the many **mezze** served in Greek and Turkish cuisines.

Associations
see: **appetizer, dolmades, hors d'oeuve, mezze**

Tart

Pronounced TART (with a as in far)

Origin
Tart derives from the Latin **torta** meaning *twisted* and also a *cake.* The word was applied to any food, usually fruit, that was very sour which tended to make one twist one's face. With time, it came to mean a pie or pastry filled with sharp flavoured fruit, such as gooseberries, rhubarb, plums and apples.

Meaning
A **tart** is an open pastry case or flan which is filled with a savoury (e.g. Swiss cheese tart) or sweet mixture (e.g. custard tart, jam tart). Sweet tarts are often eaten with cream as desserts and savoury tarts are enjoyed as snacks.

assorted tartlets

Associations

Two of the most popular tarts in France are **tarte aux prunes**
(*plum tart*) and **tarte aux pommes** (apple tart) and in
Germany **wähnen**, a *fruit tart., is very popular.* A small tart is
called a **tartlet** or, in French cuisine, a **tartine**.
see: dessert, flan , ramekin, pizza, quiche

Tartare

Pronounced TA-TA (with the a's as in far)

Origin
Tartare is French for a Tartar, a member of a clan of Turks, Russian Cossaks and some Asians, who in the 13th century under Genghis Khan terrorised Eastern Europe. They were noted for their violence. It then came to mean a person of irascible temper. It was applied to cuisine to mean a dish that attacked the taste buds, as it was sharp and strong.

Meaning
Tartare sauce, as a cold sauce, is made from mayonnaise with chopped capers, chives, gherkins and parsley added. Sometimes chopped hard-boiled eggs are included. The sauce is served with fish and croquettes. **Steak tartare** is made from raw, minced beef which is shaped into a steak and then topped with a raw egg and sprinkled with paprika. Surrounding the meat are chopped onions, capers and parsley.

Associations
Carpaccio is an Italian dish consisting of raw beef which has been marinated in oil, lemon juice and garlic. It is served with slices of parmesan cheese and pieces of raw mushrooms. **Kibbi nayga** is a Lebanese dish of raw, minced lamb mixed with burghul, chopped onion and seasoning.
see: **burghul, croquettes, mayonnaise**

Tempura

Pronounced TEM-POORA (with e as in pet, oo as in moon and a as in cat)

Origin
The Portuguese traded with Japan during the 16h century. While in Japan, they did not eat meat on Ember Days, which occur four times (**quator tempora** in Spanish) a year . On these days, they ate seafood instead, usually shrimps. The term **quator tempora** became attached to the shrimp dishes and eventually it was abbreviated to **tempura**, which became the name in Japan for dishes made with shrimps and prawns. The first specialised tempura restaurants were established in Japan in the late 19th century and have flourished ever since.

preparing tempura

Meaning
Tempura is a very popular Japanese dish consisting of strips of fish fillets or shelled and deveined shrimps and prawns (called **ebi** in Japan) and chopped vegetables, which are fried in a batter made from sifted, light flour, eggs and ice-cold water. The batter is always very cold (Heat will make it gluey.) and applied so that it will be paper-thin. The fish and seafood are fried in a wok or deep frying pan in unused, very hot, light oil until the batter has a golden crispness. The **tempura** is then served immediately, usually with a grated radish (daikòn) and ginger and a dipping sauce of dashi, soya sauce and mirin.

Associations
Lobak is a Malay dish which is similar to tempura, as is **fritto misto,** an Italian dish where fish fillets and seafood are dipped in a simple batter and fried in hot oil.
see: crustacean, dashi, mirin, soya

Photograph from " Japanese Cooking for Health and Fitness" by Kyoko Konishi, published by Gakken & Co. Ltd.

Teriyaki

Pronounced-
TERI-YAKEE (with e as in egg, i as in pin, a as in cat and ee as in see)

Origin
Yaki is Japanese for *broiling, grilling, toasting* or *baking.* **Teri** means a *glaze.* **Teriyaki** literally means *grilled with a glaze.*

Meaning

Teriyaki is a Japanese dish where meat, poultry or quite large fish are marinated in **teriyaki sauce** before being grilled and basted until the grilled food has a shining glaze. The **teriyaki sauce** is made from brewed soya sauce with the addition of mirin (or sherry), vinegar, spices (for example, grated ginger), horseradish and brown sugar. It is used as a sauce to accompany grilled meat, fish and seafood dishes, as well as being a marinade. Grated radish (such as daikon) is an excellent garnish for a teriyaki dish, as it is not only flavoursome but it also assists the digestion of oily foods.

Associations

Onigari yaki is another Japanese dish consisting of shrimps which are dipped in a sauce of mirin, soya sauce and sugar and then grilled (broiled) over hot coals.

see: garnish, marinade, mirin, soya

Terrine

Pronounced TE-REEN (with e as in pet and ee as in see)

Origin

Terrine derives from the Latin **terra** meaning *earth*. **Terrine** was originally the French for an **earthenware dish** in which meat, poultry and fish were cooked. Nowadays, the term means not only the receptacle but also the contents of the dish.

Meaning

A **terrine** is a cooked meat, poultry or fish mixture, like a **pâté**. **Duck terrine**, for example, consists of minced duck meat which is seasoned. It is blended with grated onion, chopped eggs and orange juice. The mixture is put into an oven-proof dish which is lined with slices of very fatty bacon, so that the terrine will remain moist during the time that it is being used. The mixture is pressed in the dish, so that it will be firm enough to slice when cooked and cooled. It is cooked in an oven in a shallow tin half-

pâté en croûte   pâté de campagne

a vegetable terrine

full of hot water or on a cooker in a **bain marie**. It is then left
to cool. Terrines are served cold, as an appetizer, entrée or hors
d'oeuvre. A **terrine** is also an ovenproof dish with a lid, which
allows cooking with the minimum of moisture.

Associations
**see: appetizer, bain marie, charcuterie, entreé, hors
d'oeuvre, pâté**

Timbale

Pronounced TAMBAL (with first a as in cat and second a as
in far)

Origin
Timbale derives from the Arabic **at-tabl** and later the Spanish
atabal meaning *the drum*. In French, **timbale** means a
kettledrum and in Italian a semi-spherical, small drum is
called a **timballo**. The word then came to mean a drinking cup
and bowls in the cylindrical shape of a small drum. In French
cuisine, the meaning passed, as is frequent in cuisine, from the
receptacle to the contents of the receptacle.

Meaning
A **timbale** is a small drum-shaped mould of earthenware, china
or metal which is filled with various kinds of meat or
forcemeat mixtures (e.g a ragoût, a purée or a sweetbread).

236

Traditionally, the mould is lined and then topped with a short-pastry pie crust. Sometimes, however, the timbale is baked blind and fillings(which can be very varied) are added after the crust is baked. In French cuisine, a dish made **en timbale** means that the food has been heaped into a pyramid shape onto a plate.

Associations
see: **charlotte, püree, ragoût, sweetbread**

Tofu

Pronounced TO-FOO (with o as in go and oo as in moon)

Origin
Tofu is Japanese for beancurd, which originated in China over two thousand years ago. It was introduced into Japan in the 7th century at the same time as Buddhism. At first, tofu was eaten only by the priesthood and the upper classes who associated with them.   In the early 1600's soya beans were cultivated as an additional crop to rice and by the 18th century tofu had become a popular and widely-eaten food in Japan.

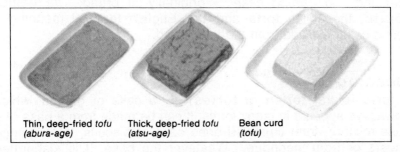

| Thin, deep-fried *tofu* (abura-age) | Thick, deep-fried *tofu* (atsu-age) | Bean curd (tofu) |

Photograph from " Japanese Cooking for Health and Fitness" by Kyoko Konishi, published by Gakken & Co. Ltd.

Meaning
Tofu is another name for *beancurd* or *soyabean curd,*, which is a staple in Japanese and Chinese cuisines. It is made from **soya beans**, which, as they are hard when raw, must be thoroughly soaked in water to soften them. They are then pounded to produce a soya bean whey. This is drained, put into a mould and heated with a solidifying agent to produce a pale-coloured, smooth-textured curd with a consistency of baked custard. It has a slightly burnt flavour, so it is an acquired taste.   It is eaten raw (usually with condiments) or is cooked. Thin rectangles or squares of

tofu which are deep fried are called **abura-age** (pronounced *abra-ag-ay*);   thick, deep-fried slices are called **atsu-age** (pronounced *atsoo-agay*). Both are eaten with rice and noodle dishes, with one-pot dishes and with miso soup. They can be opened like a pouch and filled with sushi rice or other fillings. As tofu absorbs the flavour of the food it is cooked with, it is used for both sweet and savoury dishes. All tofu is readily available from shops. It is very high in protein and calcium and low in cholesterol.

Associations
Dow foo pok is fried beancurd which is sold fresh in large cubes in China.
see: miso,   soya , sukiyaki, sushi

Torte

Pronounced TORT (with o as in port)

Origin
The German **torte** meaning a **cake** derives from the Latin **torta** meaning   *a round cake* - originally of bread. The French **tourte**, the Italian **torta** and the English **tart**, all meaning a round cake, evolved from the Latin word.

Meaning
A **torte** (plural **torten** or **tortes**) is a cake or gâteau, which nowadays appears in many forms. It can be made from a base of a cake mixture, from crumbled dried cake or biscuits, from sponge fingers or from meringue. Whatever the base, it is elaborated with creams and garnishes to produce an impressive dessert. Probably the best-known torte internationally is **sachertorte**, which was invented by Franz Sacher, the chef to Prince Metternich, the First Minister of State in Austria in 1809. He controlled Austria for 49 years. While in Vienna, he requested his chef to produce for him a dry "masculine" chocolate cake. The **Sachertorte** was the result. It is a cake with a slightly dry texture and with a   strong bitter-chocolate   flavour. It   is sometimes filled with a chocolate cream. It is usually served as a dessert with fresh or whipped cream. Another   famous   German torte is **Himmel torte** (literally *heaven torte*).

hazelnut torte

It has six layers of crisp butter biscuits, each of which is spread with a tart jelly and whipped cream. **Biscotten torte** also has layers of biscuits but they are separated by rum and almond cream and topped with thick, whipped cream which is decorated with toasted almonds. Other popular tortes are **mocha torte** (with a strong coffee flavour), **cherry torte** and **raspberry torte**.

Associations
Tortellini is a small version of **tort**. It means in Italian *a small cake* and a *fritter.* It also means rounds of pasta which are filled with a savoury mixture and then shaped around one's forefinger into a ring shape. They are then boiled in water until *al dente .* This pasta, like so many other choice dishes, originated in Bologna. **Tortells** are Spanish cakes which are rather like a doughnut. They are filled with cream or fruit and sold in cake shops.
see: al dente, dessert, gâteau, meringue, omelette

Tortilla

Pronounced TOR-TEEYA (with o as in port, ee as in see and a as in ago)

Origin

Tortilla in Spanish means an *omelette* or *pancake*. It derives from **torta** meaning a *cake.* **Tortilla** is *a little cake.* The Mexicans used the word **tortilla** to describe their particular kind of pancake. **Maize** (also called **sweet corn, Indian corn** and **corn on the cob**), from the Spanish **maiz**, is a native plant of the Peruvian Andes. It spread throughout South America into Mexico. About 5000 B.C., Mexican cuisine began with the cultivation of corn. Along with beans, chillies and tomatoes, it became a staple in the diet of the Aztecs and has remained so with Mexicans to this day.

Meaning

A **tortilla** is a round, flat, thin, unleavened pancake made from a finely-ground cornmeal dough, which is called **masa** in Spanish. It is usually toasted on a griddle. A tortilla, which is called the "bread of Mexico", is often used as a plate or a spoon. It is served in a variety of forms. A **taco**, for instance, is a tortilla which is deep fried in oil and then, using tongs, is folded over

a taco

into a thin **u** shape. It is filled with a variety of savoury mixtures and some salad. It is called the *"Spanish sandwich"* . An **enchillada** is a tortilla which is softened in oil then spread with a filling and rolled up. A **tostadas** is a tortilla which is stuffed with a filling, then folded and its edges crimped to make a package. It is fried crisp and sprinkled with chopped onions, chilli, and grated cheese or bits of meat. Small tostadas make excellent canapés. A **tamale** is a tortilla with a savoury filling, which is folded and then wrapped in a **hojas** (which is the fried husk of sweet corn) or in banana leaves and then steamed. A favourite filling for tortillas or an accompaniment to them and all other variations of the tortilla is a mash of **refried beans.**

Associations
see: **canapé, guacamole**

Tournedos

Pronounced TOOR-NAYDO (with oo as in soon, ay as in say and o as in go)

Origin
Tournedos derived from the French **tourner** meaning to turn and **dos** meaning *the back*. Today, **tournedos** is French for a *fillet of beef.* There are two versions of how the term originated and why traditionally the dish is not placed directly on the table but passed behind the back of guests. The first is that the fillet is so tender that it is cooked before the chef has time **to turn his back.** The second is that Rossini, the famous Italian composer, while at dinner in a restaurant suggested to the maître d'hôtel that the steak he was about to have for dinner should be cut, prepared and presented in a different way. The maître d'hôtel, appalled at this notion, said to Rossini that he could not possibly present a dish before him that would not conform to the accepted manner of presentation. To which Rossini replied that he would **turn his back** and not see the presentation.

Meaning
A **tournedos** is a fillet about 5 to 6 cms thick which is cut in the shape of a medallion from the centre of a whole fillet of beef. It is secured with either a skewer or cocktail stick to keep its shape

during cooking. It is fried or grilled very quickly in butter or oil to ensure that the meat remains pink inside. Before being garnished, it is sometimes placed on a small mounds of rice or on a croûton. There are hundreds of versions of tournedos which are named by the garnishes used with them. For instance, **tournedos Nicoise** is garnished with a concassé of tomatoes and **tournedos chasseur** is garnished with sautéed mushrooms, chopped shallots and a sauce of cornflour, madeira wine and seasoning. One of the best-known and most popular tournedos presentations is **tournedos Rossini**. The tournedos is arranged on a croûton which is topped with a slice of pâté

Associations
see: **croûte, fillet, garnish, medallion**

Trifle

Pronounced   TRI-FAL (with i as in bite and a as in ago)

Origin
Trifle derives from the Old English **trufle** meaning an *idle tale*,

traditional cream trifle

a *thing of no importance.* It came to mean a dish that is not hearty and substantial, like a main course but is light, like a dessert. It became a popular dessert in Britain in the late 19th century.

Meaning
A **trifle** is a rich dessert made in a large glass or porcelain dish that has a a deep, base layer of sponge cake soaked in fruit juices (or sherry wine). On this is placed a layer of fruit (canned or fresh) which in turn is covered with a layer of custard. It is topped with fresh cream. The dish is often garnished with glazed fruit and flaked chocolate

Associations
see: **dessert**

Truffle

Pronounced   TRUF-AL (with u as in trust and a as in ago)

Origin
Truffle derives from the Latin **tuber** meaning a *bump* or *knob* and the Dutch **truffel**, which describes a fungus of the genus called **tuber**. They have a long ancestry, as they were eaten in Ancient Babylon and in Ancient Rome. They were first used in French cuisine in the 14th century.

Meaning
The **truffle** is a warty, blue-black, or more rarely, a white, aromatic fungus, about the size of a golf ball. As it has no chlorophyll, it has to live parasitically with another plant, such as in the root system of certain trees. It grows underground and has to be sniffed and rooted out by trained dogs or pigs. All attempts to cultivate them have failed and it is not known why they grow in some areas attached to some plants and not others. They take several years to mature, consequently there are not many of them and they are very expensive. They are prized by gourmets in France, Italy and Spain. The finest black truffles are said to come from Périgord in South West France and the finest white truffles from Bologna in North Italy. **Périgourdine** and **périgueux** in French cuisine both mean *with ruffles* when describing a dish. Truffles do not have a distinctive taste them-

selves (They tend to be earthy.) but they are renowned as taste provokers when served with dishes such as chicken, veal, steak or lobster. They traditionally accompany pâté de foie gras. Restaurants use special graters to shave thin slices of truffle, which can be served with special (and expensive) dishes.

The term **truffle** also describes a rich, creamy chocolate dessert made from cream, dark or white chocolate, cake crumbs, ground almonds, almond essence, sultanas and raisins. A liqueur, spirit or fruit juice is added as a flavouring. By refrigeration, the paste mixture is made firm enough to mould into small balls. These are covered in chocolate vermicelli or grated chocolate.

dessert truffles

Associations

In French cuisine, **trufflée** means *stuffed with truffles.* **Tartufi** is the Italian for truffles. French truffle farmers are called **trufficulteurs.**

see: **dessert, gastronome, pâté**

Velouté

Pronounced VE-LOOTAY (with e as in pet, oo as in soon and ay as in say

Origin
Velouté is French for *velvet-like, velvety* and *downy.*

Meaning
Velouté is one of the basic sauces (**sauces méres** - or *mother sauces* - in French cuisine) and one of the three **thick soups,** the others being **cream soups** and **purées.** A **velouté** is a creamy *velvety* sauce made from a stock from fish, meat or poultry, depending upon the dish it will accompany (i.e. fish stock with a fish dish). The **liaison** (thickening) used with the sauce is a roux made of butter and flour, with sometimes a final binding of egg yolks and cream.

Associations
Sauce sûpreme is a velouté enriched with eggs and cream. **Bretonne sauce** is a velouté sauce to which celery, onions, leeks, carrots cooked in butter have been added. **Poulette and Allemande sauces** are made from velouté with a liaison of egg yolks, cream, lemon juice and chopped parsley.

see: **béchamel, bisque, chaud froid, consommé, purée, quenelle, roux, stock, sûpreme**

Vichyssoise

Pronounced VEESHY - SWAZ (with ee as in see, y as in duty, a as in far)

Origin
Vichyssoise is French for a person who lives in **Vichy,** which is a fashionable, mineral-springs watering-place at the foot of the volvanic moutains of Auvergne in Central

France. It also describes a soup which originated in the United States in the early 1900's. It was invented by an American chef whose family came from Vichy. He transformed an ordinary potato soup into a delicious cold soup.

Meaning
Vichyssoise is made from chopped leeks and onions, sliced potatoes, butter, chicken stock, nutmeg and seasoning. Having been brought to the boil, the ingredients are simmered. The soup is then sieved ,cream is stirred in and it is chilled. A blob of cream is placed on top of each serving, which is garnished with chopped chives.

Associations
see: avgolemono

Vindaloo

Pronounced
VIN-DALOO (with i as in pin, a as in ago and oo as in soon)

Origin
Vindaloo derives from the Portuguese **vinho** meaning *wine* and **alho** meaning *garlic.* **Vindaloo** was first made by portuguese settlers in Goa on the west coast of India . It was made with wine or vinegar and came to mean *vinegared.*

Meaning
Vindaloo (also spelled **bindaloo**) describes an Indian dish which is highly spiced and flavoured with **vinegar**. Vindaloo paste consists of cumin, chillies, peppercorn, cardamon, fenugreek, salt and a little sugar and tomato purée mixed to a paste with vinegar. It produces a very hot condiment, which can be used as a marinade or an ingredient for beef, lamb and pork curries. Vindaloo, Madras and Bangalore are the hottest Indian curries. **Baid vindaloo** are vinegared eggs.

Associations
see: **chilli, curry, marinade, purée**

Vitello Tonnato

Pronounced VEE-TEL-LO TON-ATO (with ee as in see, e as in pet, first o as in go and second as in on , a as in far and the final o as in go)

Origin

Vitello is Italian for a *calf* north of Florence. South of Florence the word **vitella** is used, meaning a *heifer.* In restaurants in various parts of the world, including Italy, **vitello** or **vitella** is used on menus to mean *veal, the meat from a calf.* **Tonnato** is Italian for *with tuna.* The story goes that in 1760, the cook of the Marchese Casati of Milan found herself with a problem. She was faced with unexpected guests to dinner. When the guests arrived, she had only cold, left-over veal roast and some tuna. Necessity was the mother of invention! She produced vitello Tonnato, which is now one of the most famous of Milanese dishes.

Meaning

Vitello Tonnato consists of thin fillets (or callops) of veal which are served with a sauce made from tuna, anchovy fillets, capers, lemon juice, mayonnaise and seasoning. The dish is what is described in French cuisine as a **blanquette de veau** (*veal with white sauce*). The dish is usually served with a garnish of artichoke hearts or capers and a wedge of lemon.

Associations

see: **cordon bleu, fillet, mayonnaise, saltimboca, scallopine, schnitzel**

Vol au vent

Pronounced VOL - O- VON (with first o as in doll, second as in port and third as in a naselised o in song)

Origin

Vol is French for *flying* or *flight* and **vent** for *wind,* Literally, **vol au vent** means *flight in the wind.* Probably the nearest English translation is *as light as air.*

vol au vents

Meaning

A **vol au vent** consists of a round, light, puff pastry case (with a lid which can be removed), which is filled with a savoury mixture, such as a fricassée of chicken or shellfish with a béchamel sauce, chopped goose livers or kidneys, diced mushrooms, or sweetbreads. The pastry cases are sometimes filled also with a sweet mixture. The vol au vents are usually served cold as an appetizer or as an hors d'oeuvre.

Associations

see: appetizer, béchamel, feuilletage, fricassée, hors d'oeuvre, poularde, sweetbread

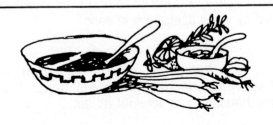

Welsh rabbit

Pronounced WELSH - RABIT (with e
as in pet , a as in apple and i as in wit)

Origin

The origin of **Welsh rabbit** reveals the
Welsh sense of humour. When Welsh
hunters had a bad day hunting and returned
home without even a rabbit, their wives
would have to produce what they called
their Welsh rabbit for dinner from what-
ever they had in their pantry - cheese. They sat down at table to
cheese on toast. Welsh rabbit became a very popular snack
dish. Some people in the mid 1700's thought it proper to refine
the dish, so they renamed it **Welsh rarebit.**

Meaning
A simple **Welsh rabbit** is melted cheese on toasted bread. A
more elaborate version is a mixture of   melted cheddar cheese to

which is added beaten egg, a little dry mustard and worcester sauce and beer. The mixture is placed on slices of bread or rusks and browned under a grill. Welsh rabbit is a popular savoury snack - or, if the hunting is poor, a main meal !

Associations
In Italy, **spiedini alla Romano** consists of cubes of bread and cheese threaded onto a skewer and then baked.

Wurst

Pronounced   VURST (with u as in cure)

Origin
Wurst is German for *sausage.*   The names of many German wursts are derived from their place of origin, such as Hamburger mettwurst, Thuringer blutwurst, Holsteiner kochwurst. The making of wurst in Germany goes back to the early 11th century.

Meaning
In Germany, Austria and Hungary there are said to be more than 300 different kinds of **wurst**, but there are four basic types of wurst: **rohwurst,** (or *dry wurst*) which is a cured, smoked or air-dried wurst, which can be eaten without cooking (e.g. **mettwurst** and **teewurst); kochwurst** (*cooked wurst*), which may be smoked but is pre-cooked and ready to eat (e.g. **leberwurst** or **liver wurst,** and **black** and **white puddings**) ; **brühwurst** (*fresh wurst*), which is smoked and scalded by the butcher and may be eaten as it is or be cooked (e.g. **frankfurters** and **bockwurst); bratwurst,** which is usually raw pork or veal with chopped onions and strong seasoning but it can be partially cooked and should be pan fried. Wurst are usually made from pork but beef wurst is also popular. Some wursts often include fairly large chunks of other meat, such as tongue or bacon. Wurst is eaten as an appetizer, a hors d'oeuvre, an entrée or as part of a main dish.

Associations
see: **appetizer, entrée, hors d'oeuvre, mortadella, sausage, sauerkraut, salami**

Yoghurt

Pronounced YOG- AT (with o as in dog and a as in ago)

Origin
Yoghurt is a Greek word which derives from the Turkish **yoghut**. Yoghurt is one of the most ancient foods in the cuisine of the Middle East, North Africa, India, and Balkan countries. According to legend, the method of making yoghurt was revealed to Abraham by an angel. Abraham, the Bible says, lived until he was 175.

Meaning
Yoghurt (also spelled **yogurt**, **yoghourt** and **yaourt**) is produced by whole or skimmed milk undergoing some fermentation by the action on it of a bacterial culture, which sours it and makes it set. The semi-solid, curd-like mixture produced (which nowadays is called **natural yoghurt**) is thick and has a sweet-sour taste. Natural yoghurt often has fruit added to it and is sweetened by sugar or a sweetening agent. The sweet yoghurt produced is used as a snack or a dessert. **Natural yoghurt** is a very important part of the diet of many countries, especially in the Middle East, India, North Africa, Greece and Turkey, where it is used as a marinade to tenderise and flavour meat and fish, is an ingredient in soups, dips and sauces, is a principal ingredient in some beverages and is much used in the making of desserts.

Associations
The Greek cake called **yaourtopita** is made from a dough of flour and yoghurt. Greece has a dip which is popular called **tzatziki**, which is made from chopped cucumber, ground garlic and yoghurt. A soup which is much enjoyed in the Black Sea area is **tarator**, which is made with yoghurt. In India, yoghurt is called **dahi**, meaning *curd.* A popular dish in India is **raytas**, which is made from yoghurt with diced fruit or vegetables and spices.
see: **dessert, dressing, felafel, korma, naan, pikelet, sweet and sour, tandoori**

Zabaglione

chocolate and coffee zabaglione

Pronounced ZABA - LEE -ONAY (with a's as in rabbit, ee as in see, o as in go and ay as in say)

Origin
Zabaglione is Italian for *egg punch.*

Meaning
Zabaglione (which is also called **zabaióne**) is a light, fluffy Italian dessert made from whisked egg yolks, fine sugar, a touch of salt and, traditionally, sweet marsala (or madeira) wine but liqueurs, champagne or even strong coffee can also be used successfully to flavour the dish. The mixture is beaten constantly over hot water in a double saucepan or bain marie, until it is thick and creamy. The heat should not be too high or the sauce will curdle. The zabaglione can be served in a glass or a coupe by itself or be a topping for fresh fruit or fruit tart . It can be poured warm over ice cream and served with sponge fingers or ratafias as a delicious dessert or as a sauce for a hot or cold pudding. In countries other than Italy, **zabaglione** is sometimes called a **wine custard**, an **egg flip** or an **egg punch**. In France, it is called a **sabayon**.

Associations
Spumone, which is Italian for *foam* or *froth*, is a delicate dessert made from whipped egg whites or whipped cream. Another wine custard or cream is **syllabub** (which was popular in England in the time of Elizabeth the First), which is made from whisked cream, wine, liqueur or cider, fine sugar and lemon juice.
see: bain marie, dessert